How to Get a
Small
Business
2nd Edition Loan

A Banker Shows You Exactly
What to Do to Get a Loan

Bryan E. Milling

Sourcebooks, Inc.
Naperville, IL

Published by Sourcebooks, Inc.
P.O. Box 372, Naperville, Illinois 60566
(630) 961-3900
FAX: (630) 961-2168

This publication is designed to provide accurate and authoritative information in regard to the subject matter covered. It is sold with the understanding that the publisher is not engaged in rendering legal, accounting, or other professional service. If legal advice or other expert assistance is required, the services of a competent professional person should be sought.

From a Declaration of Principles Jointly Adopted by a Committee of the American Bar Association and a Committee of Publishers and Associations

Library of Congress Cataloging-in-Publication Data
Milling, Bryan E.
        How to get a small business loan: a banker shows you exactly what you need to do to get a loan/ Bryan E. Milling.—2nd ed.
                p.   cm.
        Includes index.
        ISBN 1-57071-341-3   (alk. paper)
        1. Bank Loans.   2. Commercial loans.   3. Small Business—Finance.
        I. Title.
        HG1641.M454   1998
        658.15'244—dc21   98-10381
                                                CIP

Printed and Bound in the United States of America
10   9   8   7   6   5   4   3   2

To my son, Jeff, and my daughter, Karen.

Contents

Part III: How Bankers Review Business Loan Requests

Part IV: What Will You Have to Sign to Get a Loan?

Part V: What Will It Cost You to Borrow from a Bank?

Introduction

Few businesses grow and prosper without help from a commercial bank. The financial help that comes from periodic loans remains a key concern for most business managers.

One bank loan may give a business the financial boost necessary to increase its product line or expand its market area. Another loan may give a business the cash it needs to take advantage of the discounts some trade creditors offer in exchange for early payments for purchases. Still another loan may help boost a marginal sales volume up to a level that makes a business profitable.

But, no bank loan comes automatically. Your business must qualify for a bank's credit consideration. This book reviews the steps that can help your business get a bank loan.

Part 1 opens the discussion with a look at the more common types of bank loans. The different types meet different needs, so matching a particular type of loan to your need becomes an important part of any request for a bank loan.

Part 2 gives a summary view of the steps necessary to apply for a bank loan. You will find that bankers often ask for more information than you think they need. Despite that view, you must meet the banker's requests for information. Meeting those requests increases your chances of getting a bank loan.

Part 3 puts you into the banker's chair. You will see how a banker reviews business loan requests, which will help you understand why a banker approves some loan requests and denies others. Understanding the criteria that accommodate the credit decision process can also help you better manage your firm's financial circumstances. Insuring that your business can qualify for a bank loan helps increase the prospects for your firm's success.

Part 4 centers on the legal documents you have to sign to obtain a bank loan. Two categories of documents mark the distinction between the part's two chapters.

Chapter 14 first reviews the more common business loan documents. Few managers recognize the full extent of the obligations they incur when they get a bank loan. Nor do they realize the rights a bank has if they default on a loan repayment obligation.

Most managers intend to honor their bank loan obligations. Apart from that common objective, you should understand the legal obligations that arise when you get a bank loan.

Larger, more complicated bank loans raise the need for loan agreements that exceed the norm. So, chapter 15 reviews the requirements often included in loan agreements. The potential requirements will encourage you to use some thoughtful foresight. The requirements may not change, but you should understand how they can affect your business decisions.

The final part in the book helps you measure the costs you will incur when you get a bank loan. The discussion makes an important distinction between the direct cost of a bank loan and other costs that add to the real cost of borrowing. The cumulative costs can make borrowing from a bank more expensive than many managers realize.

Chapter 16 shows how to calculate the direct cost of a bank loan. The basic calculations remain simple; however, some common banking practices raise the real cost of borrowing.

Then, chapter 17 looks at several factors that can raise the total cost of a bank loan well above the apparent direct cost. Some of those costs remain unavoidable. They help provide the earnings a bank needs to provide its services. But, you can sometimes take steps to limit indirect costs associated with bank loans.

Lastly, chapter 18 shows that many managers focus too much on the costs a business incurs from bank loans. Some concern makes sense, but excessive concern about borrowing costs often obscures the benefits your business can realize from bank loans. Most often, you should focus on the actual dollar costs compared to the actual dollar benefits from a bank loan.

An important trait that sets this book apart from others is that this book does not merely offer a review of the steps necessary to get a bank loan. You will find the major ideas discussed within the chapters crystallized in a set of concise "Bank Notes." The Bank Notes help you focus on the critical ideas that can help orient your effort to get a bank loan for your business.

One Bank Note may identify a basic requirement for obtaining a bank loan. Another will help you measure the potential benefits from a bank loan. Still another may point out an essential step necessary for the successful application for a business loan.

Your situation is unique, but the need for bank credit consideration remains common to almost every independent business enterprise. You can easily adapt the Bank Notes to fit your special circumstances. You will not find every Bank Note useful, but if just one helps you get a bank loan for your business, your time with this book will be profitable.

To illustrate, the first Bank Note emphasizes an important fact:

> **Bank Note No. 1:**
> Bank loans are essential for business success.

Almost every business needs bank loans. This book can help you take the steps necessary to get a bank loan for your business. Although, even the best effort will not make the approval of any loan automatic, a thoughtful effort can increase your chances of getting a bank loan for your business.

How to Get a

Small Business Loan

Part 1

What Kind of Bank Loan Do You Need?

Chapter 1

Single Payment Loans

Banks offer several different kinds of business loans, but we can sort the more common types of bank loans into four categories:

1. Single payment loans,
2. Installment loans,
3. Lines of credit, and
4. Standby letters of credit.

This chapter reviews single payment loans. The following three chapters discuss the other types of business loans.

In each instance, you will find a review of the typical transactions that mark each type of bank loan. You also will find a review of the premises that will help you decide what option best suits you firm's needs.

Traditional Business Loans

The single payment loan represents the oldest type of bank credit consideration. A single payment loan involves only two transactions. The first occurs when the bank makes the loan. The second transaction follows on the scheduled repayment date when you repay the loan. Of course, you also must pay the bank's interest charge for the loan.

For example, you may obtain a $10,000 single payment loan from a bank for ninety days. At the end of the ninety day term, the loan and interest charges come due. A note of agreement shows your obligation to meet the scheduled repayment date.

Banks frequently make single payment loans for periods that range from thirty to one hundred eighty days. Less frequently, a single payment loan may extend for only a few days or a full year.

Using Single Payment Loans Properly

Bankers now adapt single payment loans to meet a variety of business financing needs. But, the best justification for using a single payment loan proceeds from the traditional premise—to pay for short-term needs.

> **Bank Note No. 2:**
> A single payment loan best serves a specific,
> short-term purpose.

A request for a single payment loan should identify the specific purpose for the loan and the source of the funds that will repay the loan.

Repayment may come from the anticipated completion of an installation or construction contract, or from the scheduled collection of a note receivable you have on your books. Or, it may come from the expected collection of your accounts receivable. In any event, a specific repayment source stands as a logical requirement necessary to justify a single payment bank loan.

The repayment source for a single payment loan often may not relate directly to the loan's purpose. For example, a contractor expecting a large payment from a customer in sixty days may use a single payment loan to finance the start of a new project. In this case, the loan serves a specific purpose. A predictable repayment source exists. But, the loan's purpose and the repayment source remain unrelated.

Common Purposes for Single Payment Loans

A seasonal financing requirement remains the best example of the proper use of a single payment loan. For example, a toy wholesaler may obtain a single payment loan in July to finance a seasonal increase in inventory in anticipation of the fall selling season.

The bank schedules the repayment for January when the manufacturer expects to collect payments from retailers for the toy purchases. The borrower and the banker both recognize the chain of events that raise the need for the single payment loan and provide the source of the funds for repayment.

Many businesses use single payment loans to finance seasonal financing requirements. Lawn mower, fertilizer, bathing suit, and snow ski manufacturers stand as logical examples. Single payment loans smooth the cash flows across many seasonal business cycles.

Of course, single payment loans also answer many other short-term business needs apart from a firm's seasonal financial requirements. For example, a business may use a single payment loan to:

- Finance a special buy that will be sold to produce the funds for repayment.

- Take advantage of significant discounts allowed for early payment of a large purchase.

- Solve a temporary cash flow problem caused by slow paying customers.

- Provide a temporary loan to buy fixed assets pending the arrangement of a long-term installment loan.

- Provide the funds necessary to fill an unusually large order or contract.

In any event, you and your banker should recognize the purpose for the loan and the expected source of repayment. Ignoring that requirement can create a financial problem ninety days later when the loan comes due.

When Is a Single Payment Loan Past Due?

Your banker expects you to honor all bank debt obligations promptly. Past due loans reflect poorly upon a banker's personal job performance and can become an unnecessary irritant in your relationship with your banker. Meeting debt obligations on time contributes to a successful financial partnership between a business and a bank.

Some business managers do not realize that, unlike traditional installment loans, single payment loans have no grace period beyond the scheduled maturity date. So, an unpaid single payment loan that matures on June 15 becomes past due on June 16.

> **Bank Note No. 3:**
> A single payment loan falls past due
> if not paid by its maturity date.

An occasional oversight that allows a loan to fall past due is not a serious problem, if the remedy, i.e., payment, soon follows. But, chronically ignoring loan maturity dates can injure your banking relationship.

You should not let a single payment loan fall past due if you lack the funds for payment. If a problem exists, discuss it with your banker before the loan comes due. Bankers understand problems that can affect your ability to repay a loan on time. Extensions or renewals in response to a change in circumstances are common, but bankers become less understanding when you let a loan fall past due without explanation.

Single Payment Loans with Reduction Programs

Some bankers now make single payment loans knowing that the borrower will not repay the loan in full when it comes due. Instead, a banker and a borrower may agree upon a reduction program that repays the original loan over several successive maturity dates.

To illustrate, assume a banker makes you a $50,000 single payment loan set to mature, or come due, in ninety days. However, you have no intention of repaying the loan in full when it comes due. Nor does the banker expect repayment. Instead, you and your banker have agreed upon a $10,000 quarterly reduction program. When the loan comes due in ninety days, you repay $10,000 in principal plus the accrued interest charges.

You then execute a new note agreement for $40,000, with the maturity set for ninety days later. The same reduction and renewal process recurs three more times before the final $10,000 payment retires the loan, in full, at the end of the fourth renewal period.

Many variations of this example exist. A reduction program can be tailored in a way that makes sense to you and your banker.

For example, one business may borrow $100,000, repayable in six months, to expand its inventory. The banker agrees to renew the loan in full when it matures. A reduction program then begins with principal repayments expected ninety days later. The plan creates time for the business to begin realizing the cash benefits from the higher sales expected from the expansion in inventory.

Another business may use a single payment loan to take advantage of special discounts a major supplier allows for early payment for a purchase. The business then repays the loan with periodic reductions related to its quarterly earnings.

Still another business may use several single payment loans to buy equipment to expand its operations. After completing the expansion, one large loan will consolidate the smaller loans. A single payment loan with a reduction program may become the consolidating mechanism. Or, more likely, an installment loan will consolidate the single payment loans.

No single form of credit consideration offers as much flexibility as single payment loans with reduction programs. Imagination creates the possibilities. Common sense sets the limit.

The Benefits of Single Payment Loans with Reduction Programs

Using single payment loans with reduction programs creates a combination that can benefit both businesses and banks. Businesses benefit from the opportunity to use a bank's funds for longer periods. That helps fuel expansion that might be limited without the longer term commitment of funds.

The repayment schedule set in a reduction program also simplifies a borrower's financial planning. That becomes more difficult when a business cannot look beyond the maturity date set forth in a traditional seasonal loan.

Yet, reduction programs also remain flexible borrowing arrangements. A new program, perhaps coupled with additional financing, can easily replace an existing arrangement should your circumstances change. The bank must approve of any changes. That is seldom a problem while a firm's financial circumstances and earnings remain satisfactory.

The longer term commitment implied in a reduction program also contributes toward the financial partnership between a business and a bank. Any reduction program creates a natural requirement for a banker and a business manager to work closely together.

Designing a suitable reduction program requires cooperation. Making a change in the program also requires cooperation. The interaction necessary to develop that cooperation naturally contributes to the partnership necessary for a successful banking relationship.

Combining a single payment loan with scheduled reduction programs also encourages a banker to monitor a borrower's financial condition regularly. A conscientious banker reviews a borrower's circumstances each time a loan comes up for a scheduled reduction and renewal. Should any disturbing financial trends develop, the banker can intervene before the trends become financial problems. That benefits both the bank and the borrower.

Installment Loans

A borrower repays an installment loan in a scheduled series of equal payments. The schedule usually calls for monthly payments over a long enough term to repay the loan in full.

Single payment loans remain more suitable for short-term business purposes. So, one year marks the minimum logical term for most installment loans. At the other extreme, bank installment loans can extend for five years, depending upon your needs and circumstances.

Using Installment Loans Properly

Installment loans typically have repayment schedules that extend over several years. So, such loans become most useful to finance the acquisition of assets that benefit a business for a similar term. Those assets usually have a productive life that exceeds the term of the installment loan.

> **Bank Note No. 4:**
> Installment loans usually finance
> the acquisition of productive fixed assets.

From another perspective, it makes little sense to use an installment loan, payable over several years, to gain funds for a short-term purpose. As an extreme example, assume a business obtains a $50,000 installment loan payable over five years, but the business uses the funds to solve a short-term cash flow problem. That leaves the business with a monthly payment for sixty months.

After a few months, each payment represents a sterile expenditure. The business gains no current benefit from the payment. The business must continue payments long after it realizes the benefits from the loan.

Common Purposes for Installment Loans

Using installment loans to obtain productive fixed assets is already a familiar practice to many business managers. However, as a reminder, we should look at some common examples.

Businesses typically use installment loans to:

- Purchase machinery and equipment.
- Purchase automobiles and trucks.
- Improve office or plant facilities.
- Purchase computers and telephone systems.
- Acquire other businesses.

In recent years, installment (or term) loans have also become a common source of the funds necessary to finance a firm's increasing sales volume. Let's review an example that illustrates how an installment loan meets that financing need.

Using an Installment Loan to Finance Growth

An increase in assets usually accompanies a rising sales volume in a business. A business needs a larger investment in inventory to meet the demands set by a larger sales volume, and they need more stock to produce more sales.

As sales increase, a firm's investment in accounts receivable also expands. A larger sales volume translates directly into a higher investment in accounts receivable. This remains true even though most customers honor the firm's designated credit terms.

Although the relationship is less direct, a firm's investment in other assets also increases as sales rise. An increase in sales can lead to a need for more fixed assets. The need for other business operating assets also increases. This includes the operating cash necessary to meet the daily demands that arise in every business.

In any event, a business needs to finance the rise in assets that accompanies a sales increase. Some of that financing will come from the profit embedded in its sales, and trade credit can also provide part of the financing necessary to support the growth assets. However, rapid growth raises the need for more financing than those sources can usually provide. A bank installment loan can fill that financial void. A brief look at the Panel Company illustrates that potential.

The Panel Company distributes an innovative line of wood paneling that is proving remarkably successful. The firm generated $2 million in sales during its most recent business year. Moreover, the firm expects that volume to increase by 80 percent—$3.6 million in the current year.

The Panel Company's controller recognizes the relationship between a rising sales volume and asset growth in a business. So, she wisely projects the financing requirements necessary to support that growth. That projection appears in Table 2-1.

A look at the table provides a view of the Panel Company's fiscal year-end balance sheet. At the end of the year, the firm had $1,000,000 in total assets. Trade and other creditors provided $400,000 in financing to help support those assets. The remainder of the necessary support comes from the $600,000 in stockholder's equity.

The Panel Company's controller assumes that the firm's assets will expand at the same rate as its sales. So, as shown in Table 2-1, she projects a $1.8 million asset investment by the end of the current year—an 80 percent increase. That also shows a need for $800,000 in funds to support the increase in assets.

Table 2-1: Projecting the Panel Company's Financing Needs

	Fiscal Year-End	Projected Year-End
Total Assets	$1,000,000	$1,800,000
Trade Credit	$250,000	$450,000
Other Liabilities	$150,000	$270,000
Financial Gap	—	$280,000
Stockholders' Equity	$600,000	$800,000

Part of that support can come from an increase in trade credit. A glance at Table 2-1 shows that the Panel Company's accounts payable rise by 80 percent, or $200,000, by year-end. But, no additional increase can occur without violating supplier credit terms. The Panel Company's policy calls for prompt payments to suppliers. So, that represents an unacceptable source of additional financing.

Accruals and other liabilities will also rise by $120,000 by the end of the year. The Panel Company expects to add $200,000 in retained earnings to the stockholders' equity in the business. That represents a significant reward from the higher sales volume.

However, all these sources together remain inadequate to support the Panel Company's projected increase in assets. As the Financial Gap in Table 2-1 shows, the business will need an additional $280,000 to support the projected asset expansion.

A bank installment loan, perhaps payable over three to five years, stands as a logical source of the funds necessary to fill that gap.

The funds from the loan will enable the Panel Company to preserve its reputation for credit worthiness. Also, spreading repayment over a long term will eliminate any excess pressure on the firm's cash flow. The repayment will come from the firm's future anticipated earnings. Lastly, the strong financial condition and operating profits easily qualify the firm for that credit consideration.

As a matter of contrast, the short-term repayment requirements make a single payment loan unsuitable in this instance. The required repayment would recreate the financial gap the loan originally filled.

An installment loan stands as the logical source of the funds necessary to fill that gap.

When Is an Installment Loan Past Due?

As was mentioned earlier, a single payment loan becomes past due when it remains unpaid beyond its due date. Thus, a single payment loan scheduled for repayment on November 30 becomes past due on December 1.

However, banks typically allow a grace period beyond each scheduled due date before a late installment payment falls into the past due category. The most common grace period is ten days. So, a missed payment does not appear past due until the eleventh day after the due date.

Persistent past due installment loan payments can mar the relationship between a business and a bank, so you should make all payments promptly. But, recognize that the grace period creates some flexibility for a business contending with a tight cash flow. You can be a few days late with an installment loan payment without ever appearing on a banker's past due list.

Lines of Credit

A line of credit from a bank is often a logical complement to the cash flow cycle of a business. It allows a business to readily supplement its income when cash is low and make payments when income is higher.

> **Bank Note No. 5:**
> A line of credit fluctuates
> in direct response to the peaks and valleys
> in a borrower's cash flow cycle.

Whenever a business foresees a demand for funds that will exhaust its cash reserves, a bank advances enough funds to maintain a positive cash position. Then, as the natural cash flow cycle generates funds above those needed for normal reserves, the business repays all or part of the existing bank loan.

The loan revolves as often as the peaks and valleys occur in the firm's cash flow. Figure 3-1 provides a simplified picture of that relationship. That picture gives us a view of the normal cash flow cycle in a business.

However, as suggested by the overlapping circles, the collections from the firm's accounts receivable leave it short of the cash needed to pay for purchases promptly. Foreseeing that gap, the business obtains an advance from its line of credit to get the cash necessary to maintain a prompt payment record. The eventual collections from the firm's receivables repay the advance.

Figure 3-1: Using a Line of Credit

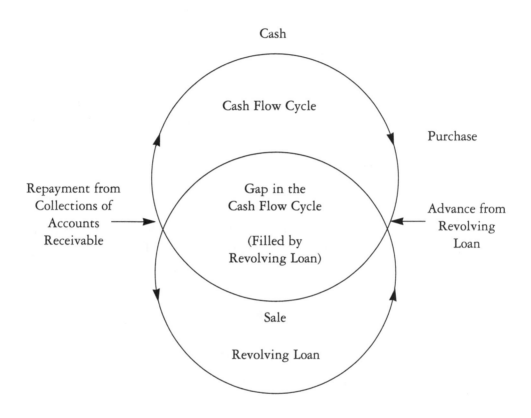

As a practical matter, lines of credit available to independent businesses typically involve the collateral pledge of the firm's accounts receivable and inventory. The loan then revolves with the movement of those assets through the business.

Common Purposes for Lines of Credit

A line of credit represents a flexible source of financing that meets several needs not served effectively by single payment or installment loans.

Some of that flexibility comes from the elimination of a predetermined repayment schedule. Of course, a revolving loan does not stand as a perpetual, open-ended arrangement. Every line of credit has a fixed date when the bank can decide whether to extend the arrangement.

In addition, banks watch lines of credit continuously. A bank can cancel the credit consideration anytime a firm's financial circumstances deteriorate. However, without severe financial setback, banks rarely cancel lines of credit suddenly.

A line of credit can do more than serve as a flexible source of funds to fill the gaps in a firm's cash flow. For example, a line of credit can become a source of expansion funds necessary for a business expecting rapid growth. If the anticipated growth does not occur, the firm does not have to draw on its line and incurs no interest expense. Yet, the arrangement insures that the funds for expansion are available if necessary.

The flexibility to borrow or not to borrow also suggests another advantage that accompanies a revolving loan. A borrower pays a simple daily interest rate for the funds used. This provides incentive for a business to borrow as little as possible and to repay as soon as possible.

As suggested above, a line of credit does not become permanent credit consideration for a business. Such arrangements have a maturity date when all outstanding advances come due. However, as long as the borrower handles the arrangement satisfactorily and remains credit worthy, banks commonly extend the arrangements.

A bank line of credit provides a flexible form of financing for a business. After a bank approves a line of credit for a business, the firm can use the funds as necessary to meet temporary gaps in its cash flow. The business then repays the advances as its cash flow improves. So, the borrower enjoys the optional use of the funds approved under the line.

Using a Line of Credit Properly

Only businesses that show significant financial strength qualify for bank lines of credit. However, that financial strength does not eliminate the need to use those lines properly.

Bank Note No. 6:
Use a line of credit to meet occasional
short-term financing requirements.

Bankers expect the balance on a firm's line of credit to fluctuate. Periodically during its term, a business should fully repay its credit line, even if the business plans to use the line again. That shows the banker that the firm is using the line properly.

Standby Letters of Credit

A bank can provide credit consideration to a business without making a loan. That occurs when a bank lends its financial strength and reputation with a standby letter of credit, guaranteeing to pay off a specific debt if the business falls delinquent.

> **Bank Note No. 7:**
>
> A bank's letter of credit guarantees payment of a specific debt obligation.

If the borrower fails to pay the debt as agreed, the obligation becomes the bank's responsibility. A standby letter of credit can be a profitable financial device useful in several common business circumstances.

First, note that a standby letter of credit places a bank's credit worthiness behind its customers. The letter becomes a guarantee that the customer will honor a specified financial obligation as agreed. If the customer fails to honor the obligation, the bank has to make the payment. A common circumstance illustrates the process.

The Local Company has a long-term relationship with the Middle National Bank. The Middle National Bank has extended many loans to the Local Company. The Local Company has repaid all of their loans as scheduled, so the Middle National Bank views the Local Company as a reliable, credit worthy enterprise.

The Local Company recently placed a $15,000 order with Apt Wholesalers, Inc., a new supplier located in a distant state. Lacking any previous experience, Apt Wholesalers is reluctant to extend the Local Company $15,000 in open account credit on its normal thirty day terms.

Of course, Apt Wholesalers could require prepayment for the purchase or cash payment on delivery. But, either choice would create an undesirable strain on the Local Company's cash flow.

So, the Middle National Bank issues a standby letter of credit that solves both companies' problems. More precisely, Middle National Bank issues a $15,000 letter of credit in favor of Apt Wholesalers, Inc., for the benefit of the Local Company. The letter provides the bank's irrevocable guaranty for the Local Company's $15,000 purchase from Apt Wholesalers on its standard thirty day terms. The Local Company remains an unknown entity to Apt Wholesalers, but Apt can easily verify that the Middle National Bank is a sound financial institution.

After receiving the letter of credit, Apt can make the $15,000 sale to the Local Company on its normal thirty day terms. Should the Local Company fail to honor those terms, Apt Wholesalers can obtain payment directly from the Middle National Bank.

From the supplier's perspective, the Middle National Bank's letter of credit eliminates the credit risk associated with the sale to the Local Company. The letter shifts that risk onto the Middle National Bank. Should the Local Company fail to pay the supplier within the agreed terms, the obligation becomes the bank's responsibility.

Of course, from the bank's perspective, the $15,000 financial obligation arising from the transaction ultimately remains with the Local Company. Presumably, the Local Company will pay for the $15,000 purchase from Apt Wholesalers within the agreed terms. That payment then dissolves Apt Wholesalers' right to draw against the Middle National Bank's letter of credit.

Should the Local Company fail to make the $15,000 payment on time, Apt Wholesalers will request the payment from the Middle National Bank. But, the bank's payment comes from the proceeds of a $15,000 loan to the Local Company. The Local Company then must repay the bank's loan, with interest, when scheduled.

So, in either circumstance, the Local Company remains responsible for the $15,000 payment for the purchase from Apt Wholesalers. The Local Company can pay for the purchase directly, or the Local Company can repay the bank loan that results when the Middle National Bank has to honor its irrevocable letter of credit.

The Local Company's financial responsibility in this instance deserves special attention. To qualify for a letter of credit, a business must satisfy the credit criteria necessary to qualify for a loan in the same dollar amount. The bank must rely on the business as the source of repayment for any potential draw against a letter of credit.

Some business managers assume that a bank incurs no risk from issuing a letter of credit. If a customer pays the supplier, the seller never draws on the letter of credit. Presumably, a business unable to qualify for a $15,000 direct bank loan still may qualify for a $15,000 letter of credit issued for its benefits.

But, a bank letter of credit remains irrevocable. A bank cannot withdraw its commitment to honor a letter of credit. Nor can any banker be sure that no draw will ever occur on a letter of credit. So, bankers view the request for a letter of credit in the same way as a request for a direct loan. The same criteria governs the credit decision process. A business that does not qualify for a bank loan will not qualify for a bank's letter of credit. A bank issues standby letters of credit only for credit worthy borrowers.

> **Bank Note No. 8:**
> Bankers view a standby letter of credit
> as if it were a loan.

The potential financial exposure from a loan and a standby letter of credit remains the same. A business unable to qualify for one will remain unable to qualify for the other.

Now, let's review the benefits that result from the letter of credit issued for the Local Company.

First, the letter of credit helped avoid unnecessary strain on the Local Company's cash flow. The letter of credit enabled the firm to delay making the $15,000 payment for the purchase from Apt Wholesalers for thirty days.

Of course, the Local Company could borrow the necessary $15,000 from the Middle National Bank and pay cash for the purchase, since a business that qualifies for a $15,000 letter of credit also qualifies for a direct bank loan in the same amount. But, using a letter of credit instead of a loan offers some cost advantages. To illustrate, let's compare the cost of a $15,000 thirty day loan to the cost for a letter of credit issued for thirty days.

First, assume the bank will charge a 10 percent annual interest rate for the $15,000 loan. That represents a $1,500 interest charge for a full year. The loan in this instance would extend only thirty days, so the charge becomes one-twelfth of the annual charge, or $125.

The charge for issuing letters of credit varies among banks. But as a typical example, many banks charge $1-1^{1}/_{2}$ percent per year of the face value of a letter of credit. Banks prorate that charge for letters that cover periods shorter than one year.

In this instance, a business must pay $225 for a $15,000 bank letter of credit issued for a full year. That drops to only $18.75 for a $15,000 letter of credit that expires in thirty days. That cost is significantly below the cost of a loan for the same amount.

Sometimes, using a standby letter of credit can create another cost benefit for a business. That occurs when a buyer negotiates price reductions from a supplier in exchange for the payment guarantee that comes from a letter of credit. After all, a letter of credit eliminates the financial risk the supplier incurs from selling to a customer on normal credit terms. Some suppliers will recognize that fact by lowering their prices.

However, do not wait for suppliers to offer that consideration. Make the price break stand as a logical consideration for providing a bank letter of credit to secure your payment.

Apart from any potential price concessions, using letters of credit simplifies the creation of a relationship with new suppliers. The ability to provide a bank's letter of credit provides clear testimony about a firm's credit worthiness. When coupled with prompt payment for purchases, a business can more readily develop open lines of credit with new suppliers.

The Local Company's experience illustrates the most common use of bank standby letters of credit. But, we should also note that standby letters of credit also serve other useful business purposes.

A construction company may use a standby letter of credit to enhance its bonding capacity, i.e., the insurance that supports its ability to complete a contract. A real estate concern may use a standby letter of credit to secure a piece of property pending completion of financing. Another business may use a letter of credit as partial collateral for a longer term debt obligation. That collateral may enable the business to receive a lower rate on the loan, which easily offsets the cost of the letter of credit.

A standby letter of credit becomes useful in any business circumstance where a prospective creditor needs additional evidence of another's financial capability. Standby letters of credit can provide that evidence at a modest cost that makes them useful commercial devices. When used properly, they can also become profitable for a business.

Part II

How to Apply for
a Bank Loan

Preparing a Request for a Bank Loan

No bank or banker approves every loan request, so prudent business managers take steps to increase the potential for a positive response. In any circumstance, a well-prepared request increases the potential for obtaining a bank loan.

A Sensible Business Purpose

A logical business purpose should justify a business loan request. That requirement may appear obvious, because a business need usually spurs the request for a bank loan.

> **Bank Note No. 9:**
> A sensible business purpose
> must justify the request for a bank loan.

Although the requirement for a sensible business purpose may appear obvious, some business managers make loan requests based on the vague premise that they can make money with the bank's money. That presumably eliminates the need to specify a purpose for the bank loan.

Yet, that need always exists. Bankers make loans to meet specific business needs. Requesting a bank loan without a well-defined purpose almost guarantees a negative response.

Of course, by itself, a sensible purpose is not enough to justify a bank loan. A borrower must also satisfy a bank's other credit criteria. But, the absence of a clearly defined purpose for a bank loan invites declination whatever a firm's financial circumstances.

Financial Statements

Copies of your firm's current financial statements should accompany every loan request. Current financial information includes up-to-date business balance sheets and income statements.

Those accounting documents respectively provide a view of your firm's current financial circumstances and a measure of your recent financial progress. Responsible lenders do not make lending decisions without the information that comes from those financial statements.

A banker also needs a look at your firm's historical financial data. That should include a review of your firm's financial circumstances as presented in its fiscal year-end balance sheet for the most recent three years. Year-end income statements covering the same number of years are also a normal requirement.

A look at those financial statements gives lenders a historical perspective of a firm's operations. That perspective provides the basis for evaluating a firm's prospects for surviving the economic vagaries inherent in an uncertain future.

In no circumstance should you hide derogatory financial information. Bankers understand that businesses sometimes have financial problems. So, revealing such problems does not necessarily lead to the denial of a loan request. However, an effort to hide the problems will often cause a banker to deny the request.

Bankers may also ask for copies of your firm's tax returns for the past three years. A look at those returns help reassure the banker that the accounting documents represent the firm's financial circumstances.

The request for copies of tax returns most often arises when you make your first request for a bank loan. The returns provide the credibility that can help cement a new relationship.

A request for tax returns seldom arises when you can provide financial statements audited by certified public accountants. Audited statements verify the financial view of a firm's circumstances. However, since the expense associated with producing audited statements remains prohibitive for many independent businesses, providing copies of tax returns is usually simpler and less costly.

Personal Financial Statement

Independent businesses often operate as corporations. Incorporation makes a business a separate legal entity from the shareholders who own stock in the corporation. Of course, the typical independent corporation usually has only a few shareholders. Most often, one shareholder holds controlling interest.

Several reasons justify incorporating a business, but limiting the liability of the shareholders usually figures prominently in the decision. Since it stands as a separate entity, the corporation's liabilities do not become liabilities for the business owners, i.e., the shareholders. That seldom holds true when businesses seek bank credit consideration, because often the bank will ask the major shareholder to sign a personal guaranty.

> **Bank Note No. 10:**
> A personal guaranty by the major shareholder stands as a common requirement for bank credit consideration.

Signing a personal guaranty removes the limits on the financial liability the controlling shareholder may expect from the corporate veil. The guarantor becomes personally liable if the corporation cannot repay the bank's credit consideration.

Bankers can easily justify that requirement. After all, a firm's major shareholder becomes the real beneficiary of the corporate benefits that come from a bank loan. Logically, the shareholder should also become liable if the corporation loses the capacity to repay the bank's loan.

Given that view, a prospective guarantor's personal financial statement should also accompany a firm's request for a bank loan. Bankers may also want copies of a guarantor's recent personal income tax returns. On occasion, a guarantor's personal financial circumstances can become a factor in the decision to approve or deny a request for a bank loan.

Other Financial Information

Financial statements provide a view of a firm's history. However, many bankers will also have an interest in a prospective borrower's future financial prospects. So, they will request at least two complementary projections.

One projection forecasts the results a firm expects from its future operations. That forecast will typically proceed monthly for the next twelve months. Longer term projections may extend on a quarterly or annual basis for as many as five years.

The other financial forecast projects a firm's anticipated cash flows. Again, the projections usually show monthly cash flows for the upcoming twelve months. Then, projections on a quarterly or annual basis may follow.

Most business managers have access to the financial statements that show their past operating results. But, the steps necessary to develop financial and cash flow forecasts often seem more elusive. The following chapter provides a look at the steps that enter the completion of those forecasts.

Before turning to that discussion, note that the information discussed in this section is common for most business loan requests. However, many loan requests will raise the need to provide more material to help justify a bank loan.

In one instance, that will call for information on the value of collateral that may secure a bank loan. Or, a banker may want to look at purchase orders or contracts to verify a projected sales increase. In another instance, a banker may want to see a comprehensive business plan.

Generally, provide whatever information your banker requests. If the banker wants the information to justify making a loan, you probably need the information to manage your business more effectively. Reluctance to provide additional information only makes it less likely that a bank will approve your request for a loan.

Step-by-Step Financial Forms

Few independent business managers operate comfortably with the fundamental accounting process. The accounting detail necessary to measure a firm's financial progress and evaluate its financial condition repels most managers. Financial and cash flow forecasts stand as even less enchanting tasks.

Nevertheless, a banker's lending decision proceeds from the financial view displayed in conventional business balance sheets and income statements that conform to Generally Accepted Accounting Principles (GAAP). Those principles define the language that enables lenders to analyze a firm's financial circumstances.

Historical and Pro Forma Statements

Financial statements provide a historical summary of a firm's operations. Bankers rely on a firm's balance sheets and income statements as the foundation for the business credit decision process.

However, bankers expect future projections as a logical complement to a borrower's historical financial statements. Those projections help anticipate the results from a firm's future operations.

Some managers view pro forma forecasts with disdain. They argue that an uncertain future makes any financial forecast futile.

Vagaries that affect every business presumably make a forecast invalid before the ink dries. However, bankers believe that valid premises for financial forecasts exist.

The Need for Financial Forecasts

Financial forecasts can make a valuable contribution to effective business management. Indeed, the manager without financial forecasts operates at a competitive disadvantage.

First, the forecasting process helps anticipate competing demands on a firm's limited resources. Those demands remain inevitable in any instance, but a common trait among independent business managers exacerbates the problem.

Those managers typically have ambitions that far exceed the limits set by their firms' resources. Some want growth that exceeds those limits. Others want to commit funds to new product development when the firm's normal operations have a better claim on the funds. The financial forecasting process provides the opportunity to analyze competing demands and set the priorities that help allocate the limited resources in a prudent, profitable manner.

As part of the process, you should also examine your own customer base. That helps insure that the forecast enables your business to continue serving those customers. You should step back and examine the competition and your firm's place in the competitive environment. The forecast should also allocate adequate resources for attracting new customers. The failure to anticipate either need can become an obstacle to continuing success.

An effective financial forecast also leads to an analysis of your business. A thoughtful effort will analyze your organization and operational structure. That effort may lead to changes that improve your operations.

In addition, the financial forecasting process becomes a logical time to review your business strategy. Changes in products, competitors, or markets may call for changes in that strategy. The final forecast should anticipate the effects of any changes.

Note that performing these analyses in any single year does not preclude the need to repeat the analysis during each successive forecasting period. A changing environment can easily make last year's analysis obsolete. The failure to do a regular analysis leaves you at the mercy of more thoughtful, more aggressive competitors.

The traditional premises still provide the primary benefits a business gains from a forecast. A forecast helps set the standard for measuring, evaluating, and controlling a firm's performance. Starting with sales, the forecast identifies the goals that can orient the efforts of all employees and managers in a business enterprise.

As you proceed through the business year, the monthly and quarterly goals set forth in the forecast provide the standards for evaluating your firm's performance. Achieving or exceeding forecasted objectives becomes a sign of management success.

From the opposite perspective, a forecast becomes a valuable management tool when your actual sales or expenses depart from projections. The numbers in a financial forecast provide standards for evaluating performance, and when necessary, those numbers also provide the basis for corrective actions. Without a forecast, you lack any criteria for evaluating your firm's performance. You also lack the basis for positive management actions to keep a firm on track. When used properly, a financial forecast serves as a management rudder that helps guide a business through an uncertain economic environment.

The whole forecasting process stems from a sales forecast, and no sales forecast stems from perfect prescience. Actual results always depart to some extent from projections, but developing targets in a forecast still provides valuable criteria for evaluating a firm's performance. The absence of those criteria leaves management blind.

Despite common fears, a forecast does not become a rigid, restrictive accounting tool that limits your management actions. Financial forecasts remain flexible devices that you can adjust in response to actual operating results. Putting a forecast in place provides criteria for adapting to changing circumstances.

In any event, the discussion here only provides an overview of the benefits a business derives from conscientious financial forecasting. Undoubtedly, the process remains challenging. The process is also a tedious accounting task, but the benefits easily compensate for that effort. The business that uses financial forecasts builds a management foundation that provides the basis for growth and prosperity.

The Elements of a Financial Forecast

The step-by-step process necessary to complete a comprehensive financial forecast exceeds the province of this discussion. Use a competent accountant to help develop the financial forecast for your business.

A complete financial forecast will include:

1. A profit (loss) projection,

2. A cash flow forecast, and

3. Projected pro forma balance sheets.

The following discussion explains the need for these three complementary forecasts and provides some illustrative formats for the projections.

A Profit (Loss) Projection

Every financial forecast begins with a projection of a firm's expected profits (or losses). An effective forecast will divide a firm's expected sales, expenses, and operating results into logical intervals useful for management.

Most forecasts proceed monthly. Using a monthly financial forecast can help identify opportunities to reverse losses in particular months or improve profits in other months. A monthly financial forecast can become a proactive management tool.

Table 6-1 provides a format for an annual Forecast of Profit (Loss) developed monthly. Expense categories for different businesses vary, so Table 6-1 only suggests a format for the basic profit (loss) forecasting process.

In any event, projected earnings represent only one element in a firm's financial forecast. A cash flow projection also stands as an essential financial planning tool. However, note some logical precepts. Financial planning begins with a sales forecast. You must project your anticipated sales volumes as precisely as possible. As suggested above, that forecast should project the sales your business can expect monthly. That schedule remains a logical prelude to developing an efficient purchase and production schedule.

The specific steps necessary to produce a sales forecast vary among businesses. As a business grows larger, sales forecasting can become a complex task that requires special expertise. However, we should note an important consideration that affects the sales forecasting process.

Every sales forecast inevitably contains a margin of error. The variables inherent in a volatile economy make precise prediction impossible. However, this lack of precision does not eliminate the value of a sales forecast or the benefits a business derives from financial planning. Those benefits develop despite a significant margin of error in the sales forecast. A questionable forecast that helps you consider your future prospects serves as an invaluable management tool.

In any event, projected sales, expenses, and income represent only one element in a firm's financial forecast. A complementary cash flow projection also stands as an essential management tool.

Cash Flow Forecast

Some business managers find the need for both a financial forecast and a forecast of extraneous cash flow. Many find them redundant. That view ignores the difference between the accounting measure of a firm's financial transactions and the related cash transactions.

After all, the typical business seldom generates a sale directly in exchange for cash. Instead, the firm trades its products in exchange for its customers' promises to pay for the purchase according to the designated selling terms.

You typically make purchases on credit similarly. In either event, cash payment usually follows the actual purchase (or sale) by thirty days.

The accrual accounting process often creates confusion since it does not distinguish between the timing of financial and cash transactions. On the seller's side, a financial transaction records a sale on the day it occurs, although no cash changes hands. Again, a sale on credit exchanges a product or service for the customer's promise to pay later. Similarly, a buyer records a purchase and an increase in accounts payable at the time the transaction occurs, but the financial record of the transaction does not affect either the buyer's or the seller's cash until the promised payment follows. This process often appears more confusing because the accrual accounting process also requires ledger entries that reflect the expected exchange of cash that completes a sale.

Table 6-1: Forecast of Profit (Loss)

	Historical Monthly Average OR Industry Comparison	1st	2nd	3rd
1. Total Sales (net)				
2. Cost of Sales*				
3. Gross Profit (line 1 - line 2)				
Expenses				
4. Salaries (other than Owner)				
5. Payroll Taxes				
6. Rent				
7. Utilities (including phone)				
8. Professional Services (accountant)				
9. Taxes & Licenses				
10. Advertising				
11. Supplies (for business)				
12. Office Supplies				
13. Interest (loans, contracts)				
14. Insurance				
15. Depreciation				
16. Travel (incl. operating vehicle)				
17. Entertainment				
18. Dues & Subscriptions				
19.				
20.				
21. Total Expenses (add lines 4–20)				
22. Profit before Taxes (line 3 - line 21)				

* Line 2—Cost of Sales: Retail—Beginning Inventory Plus Purchases, Minus Ending Inventory. Manufacturing—Cost of Material Plus Labor

Financial accounting enables a business to measure its financial performance by matching its revenues and expenses as they occur. But, accrual accounting does not reflect a firm's actual cash flow. This picture comes from the record of cash receipts and payments that record the exchange of cash that results from a sale.

	4th	5th	6th	7th	8th	9th	10th	11th	12th	TOTAL

Expenses

An exchange of cash completes a business transaction. It represents a customer's payment for a purchase or your payment for your own firm's obligation. The record of cash receipts and disbursements reflects the timing of the cash flow into and out of a business. This record provides the proper picture of a firm's cash flow. That holds true even though the accounting measure of a firm's financial transactions seldom coincides with the cash payments that complete a purchase or sale.

So, a cash budget anticipates the timing of the cash receipts and disbursements expected for a business, and projects the firm's expected cash flow as distinct from the financial accounting process that measures the ultimate results of those transactions.

Table 6-2 provides a format for developing a Forecast of Cash Flow for a business. Use it as a logical management complement to the financial Forecast of Profit (Loss), shown earlier in Table 6-1. Both are essential tools for effective business management.

Table 6-2: Forecast of Cash Flow

	Historical Monthly Average OR Industry Comparison	1st	2nd	3rd
Income				
1. Cash Sales				
2. Collection of Accounts Receivable				
3.				
4. Other Income (Add lines 1–3)				
Disbursements				
5. Owner's Salary				
6. Loan Repayments (Principal)				
7. Cost of Sales (line 2 from Table 6-1)				
8. Total Expenses (minus line 16 from Table 6-1)				
9. Capital Expenditures (Equipment, Bldg., Leasehold Imp.)				
10. Reserve for Taxes				
11.				
12. **Total Disbursements** (add lines 5–11)				
13. **Cash Flow Monthly** (line 4 minus line 12)				
14. Cash Flow Cumulative (line 13 + line 14 of prev. month)				

Pro Forma Balance Sheets

The third element in a complete financial forecast comes from a set of projected pro forma balance sheets. The projected balance sheets show the firm's anticipated financial condition for the upcoming two or three years. Some bankers will want quarterly pro forma balance sheets.

Table 6-3 shows the basic components that make up a business balance sheet. Current assets come first on the assets side of the balance sheet. Current liabilities head the list of a firm's liabilities. Accounts described as "current" refer to a time less than or equal to one year. Current assets are generally cash or will become cash within a year. Current liabilities are obligations that must be paid within a

	4th	5th	6th	7th	8th	9th	10th	11th	12th	TOTAL
Income										
Disbursements										

year. Locating the current assets and current liabilities in this manner helps you quickly assess a firm's liquidity.

Fixed assets fall into a different category from a firm's current assets. Fixed assets include a firm's property, plant, and equipment.

Table 6-3: Business Balance Sheet

December 31, 1998

Current Assets		Current Liabilities	
Cash	$ 5,000	Accts. Payable	$10,000
Accts. Rec.	15,000	Note Payable	10,000
Inventory	20,000	Long-Term Liabilities	5,000
Fixed Assets	10,000		
		Total Liabilities	$25,000
		Stockholders' Equity	
		Paid-in-Capital	$10,000
		Retained Earnings	15,000
		Total Stockholders' Equity	25,000
Total Assets	$50,000	Total Liab. + Equity	$50,000

Besides current liabilities, a business often has obligations that are due more than a year from the balance sheet date. Such liabilities then stand apart as long-term liabilities.

The stockholders' equity consists of paid-in capital (the owners' original investment in the business) and retained earnings. Retained earnings represent the portion of the income that the firm has earned over the years that it retains to support future operations.

The need for pro forma balance sheets escapes some business managers. They presume that projected earnings coupled with cash flow budgets should be sufficient for a bank's credit decision process.

However, a profitable business does not necessarily maintain a sound financial condition. Even a profitable business can accumulate an excessive debt burden that can threaten its survival. Pro forma balance sheets help bankers (and managers) anticipate such problems.

Part III

How Bankers Review Business Loan Requests

Chapter 7

Financial Credit Criteria

Obviously, no request for a bank loan receives automatic approval. You must meet a bank's credit criteria to qualify for a loan.

Understanding a bank's credit criteria should improve communications between you and your banker. If you understand your banker's perspective, you can respond better to his or her questions about your firm's circumstances. You will also better understand the response to any loan request.

Recognizing a bank's credit criteria can also contribute to your financial management efforts. Qualifying for a bank loan shows that your business enjoys current financial stability and encouraging prospects for the future.

Also, insuring that your business qualifies for a bank loan, necessary or not, helps protect against unforeseen financial setbacks. A business that remains qualified for a bank loan is more likely to prosper.

Of course, different credit criteria exist among banks. One bank may grant a loan another refuses. So, after reviewing the criteria that generally orient bank credit decisions, we touch on the factors that lead one bank to approve a loan that other banks decline.

The Basic Analysis

The specific financial criteria that qualify a business for a bank loan vary with the circumstances. Differences among businesses and among banks inevitably alter the emphasis placed on different financial considerations. However, most banks use two sets of comparative financial criteria to orient their credit analyses:

  1. Internal comparative criteria, and

  2. Industry comparative criteria.

The discussion below illustrates how these comparative criteria enter a bank's credit analysis. However, an important fact about the industry comparative criteria used in a bank's credit analysis deserves mention.

Banks typically use comparative criteria from companies with similar operating characteristics. After all, it makes little sense to compare a privately-owned local firm with a $1 million annual sales volume to a public national concern producing $1 billion in sales annually. Financial guidelines appropriate for one seldom fit the other.

Table 7-1: Balance Sheet for the Sample Corporation

Cash	$ 50,000	
Accounts Receivable	175,000	
Inventory	150,000	
Total Current Assets		$375,000
Factory Building	$ 75,000	
Machinery (Net of Dep.)	50,000	
Total Fixed Assets		$125,000
Total Assets		$500,000
Accounts Payable	$100,000	
Note Payable	50,000	
Other Current Liabilities	25,000	
Total Current Liabilities		$175,000

(Table 7-1 cont'd)	
Long-Term Liabilities	75,000
Total Liabilities	$250,000
Common Stock	$100,000
Retained Earnings	150,000
Total Stockholders' Equity	$250,000
Total Liabilities and Equity	$500,000

Many banks use the Annual Statement Studies prepared by Robert Morris Associates (RMA) as the source of comparative financial data for independent businesses. RMA compiles the financial information included in its annual publication from data provided by its member bank loan and credit officers.

Making comparison the primary criterion for financial analysis undoubtedly lacks precision. But, comparative financial analysis remains the foundation for a bank's evaluation of a firm's credit worthiness.

The sections that follow focus on the major financial criteria that orient a bank's credit analysis. We will use the most current balance sheet for the Sample Corporation (Table 7-1) as one basis for the discussion.

The discussion of a bank's internal comparative analysis also refers to the Sample Corporation's fiscal year-end balance sheets for the past three years. However, a look at those balance sheets is not necessary.

Three Critical Criteria

The influence a firm's financial circumstances exert on a bank's credit decisions comes from three primary considerations:

> 1. Liquidity,
>
> 2. Financial strength, and
>
> 3. Profitability.

Many other considerations can overcome negative aspects that appear in any part of a bank's credit analysis of a prospective borrower, but the three financial factors discussed here remain prominent in any circumstance.

Liquidity

A firm's financial liquidity stands as a prominent aspect of any credit analysis. Liquidity analysis addresses two concerns.

First, a firms liquidity level provides an estimate of its ability to meet its current obligations as they come due. An inadequate level of liquidity widens the spectrum of potential problems that can arise when a business defaults on its obligations. An adequate level of liquidity stands as a logical prerequisite to qualify a business for a bank loan.

Bankers also remain concerned with a prospective borrower's ability to absorb unforeseen financial setbacks. A high level of liquidity augments that ability. A financial setback becomes more severe in a business with a low level of financial liquidity.

Banks typically use two common criteria to evaluate the level of financial liquidity in a business enterprise—current ratio and quick ration.

> **Bank Note No. 11:**
> The current ratio serves as the primary criterion for managing a firm's liquidity.

Current Ratio

The current ratio relates a firm's current assets to its current liabilities:

Current Ratio $=$ $\dfrac{\text{Current Assets}}{\text{Current Liabilities}}$

Using the totals included in the Sample Corporation's balance sheet in Table 7-1, we find:

Current Ratio $=$ $\dfrac{\$375,000}{\$175,000}$ $=$ 2.14

The Sample Company's current ratio suggests that the firm has enough liquid assets to meet its short-term obligations 2.14 times. That exceeds the 2.0 current ratio that represents the traditional mark of an adequate level of liquidity for a business. Of course, the credit analysis process also compares that ratio to the current ratios for the business in past years.

In this instance, the bank can compare the 2.14 current ratio to that found in the firm's fiscal year-end balance sheets for the previous three years:

The Sample Corporation's Comparative Current Ratios

Year 3	Year 2	Year 1	Current Year
2.62	2.46	2.27	2.14

Although the Sample Corporation's 2.14 current ratio remains satisfactory in comparison with the traditional standard, we now see that the firm's current ratio, and its financial liquidity, has been declining for three years.

At first glance, the trend appears disturbing. The persistent decline in liquidity implies some erosion in the Sample Corporation's ability to meet its current obligations. However, such trends often have sound justification. The Sample Corporation might have previously carried an excess investment in accounts receivable or inventory that inflated the firm's current assets.

The downward trend may represent the result of more effective management of the firm's current assets. In either event, a complete credit analysis looks at the forces behind a firm's financial trends.

A bank's credit analysis also includes a comparison of a firm's ratios with external industry standards. The comparison for the Sample Corporation is:

Sample Corporation Current Ratio	Industry Average Current Ratio
2.14	1.8

The Sample Corporation's current ratio stands significantly above the industry average. That suggests that the firm has an adequate level of liquidity. That comparison also lends support to the positive perspective of the downward trend in the firm's liquidity apparent in internal trend analysis.

Again, we lack all the information necessary to draw any conclusions, but this discussion provides a sense of the process banks use to analyze a firm's financial circumstances.

A similar comparison looks at other ratios developed from the financial information in a firm's balance sheets and income statements.

The Quick Ratio

A business with a current ratio that appears satisfactory still may lack an adequate level of liquidity. That apparent contradiction develops when the composition of a firm's current assets or current liabilities becomes unbalanced. The comparative view of two businesses illustrates the potential problem:

	Company X	Company Y
Cash	$ —	$ 7,500
Accounts Receivable	—	7,500
Inventory	20,000	5,000
Total Current Assets	$20,000	20,000
Accounts Payable	$ —	$20,000
Notes Payable	10,000	3,000
Accrued Liabilities	—	2,000
Total Current Liabilities.	$10,000	$10,000
Current Ratio	2.0	2.0

The equal current ratios suggest that both firms enjoy the same degree of liquidity. However, the comparative composition of each firm's current assets and liabilities make it apparent that Company Y has a much higher level of liquidity. The firm's cash and accounts receivables provide a significant degree of liquidity compared to Company X's single investment in inventory.

Moreover, Company Y's liabilities represent a comfortable distribution of obligations compared to Company X's single liability. Company X's 2.0 current ratio in this instance clearly does not represent an adequate level of liquidity.

> **Bank Note No. 12:**
> The acid-test (quick ratio)
> stands as a more stringent test
> of a firm's liquidity.

The quick ratio is similar to the current ratio, but it excludes inventory from consideration as liquid asset:

$$\text{Quick Ratio} = \frac{\text{Cash} + \text{Accounts Receivable}}{\text{Current Liabilities}}$$

Using the date for the Sample Corporation in Table 7-1, we find:

$$\text{Quick Ratio} = \frac{\$50,000 + \$175,000}{\$175,000} = \quad 13$$

The quick ratio makes an obvious contribution to the estimate of a firm's liquidity. Inventory represents a firm's least liquid major assets. So, the quick ratio stands as a better measure of a firm's immediate ability to meet its obligations from cash on hand and collections from its accounts receivable.

Of course, a look at comparative internal and industry ratios remains necessary to draw any conclusions about the Sample Corporation's quick ratio. That comparison would proceed in a manner analogous to that discussed previously for the current ratio.

Financial Strength

A business with an adequate level of liquidity can meet its immediate obligations as they come due. However, the business that enjoys an adequate level of liquidity still may lack the underlying financial strength necessary to justify bank credit consideration. That strength must come from the financial commitment that comes from the stockholders' or owner's equity in a business.

> **Bank Note No. 13:**
> The debt-to-equity ratio evaluates
> a firm's financial strength.

The debt-to-equity ratio relates the borrowed funds a business uses to the accounting measure of the stockholders' investment in the business. To illustrate, we again use the information included in the Sample Corporation's balance sheet in Table 7-1:

$$\text{Debt-to-Equity} = \frac{\text{Total Debt}}{\text{Total Equity}}$$

$$\text{Debt-to-Equity Ratio} = \frac{\$250,000}{\$250,000} = 1.0$$

The Sample Corporation uses one dollar in borrowed funds for each dollar that comes from shareholders. That falls within the two-to-one traditional standard that marks the limit on the debt burden an independent business should carry. A lower debt-to-equity ratio implies a higher level of financial strength. A higher ratio can disqualify a business from bank credit consideration.

The two-to-one standard does not become an arbitrary standard. Experience with many businesses over many years proves that businesses with higher ratios tend to develop financial problems. Banks extending credit consideration to those businesses will sustain an unacceptable level of losses from loans that become uncollectible.

Of course, the traditional limit is not appropriate for every business. So, the credit analysis again must look at industry standards and internal comparative trends.

A couple of premises justify a bank's critical view of a firm's debt-to-equity ratio.

First, a bank views the equity in a business as the first line of defense against any financial setbacks a borrower might incur. The traditional requirement for a two-to-one ratio helps insure that the business has the financial ability to absorb any losses that develop from that setback. Financial strength also becomes the foundation for recovery.

The second premise that makes a higher debt-to-equity ratio unacceptable to a bank proceeds from a realistic view of human nature. Bankers realize that many borrowers lack concern about protecting a lender's interests. So, as debt rises compared to a firm's equity, many managers tend to exercise less management caution. Risk becomes more acceptable when creditors will suffer the larger loss from a management mistake. From a banker's perspective, requiring at least one dollar in equity for every two dollars loaned by creditors helps discourage that attitude.

Profitability

An adequate level of liquidity suggests that a business can meet its current obligations. Financial strength provides a business with the ability to absorb losses without raising the possibility of failure. However, to obtain a bank loan, a business also must show a history of profitable operations.

No example of what makes up an adequate level of profits for a business exists. You can measure and evaluate a firm's profit margins; you can examine changes in profits from one year to the next year; but you cannot define an adequate level of profits in absolute terms.

But, remember that your firm's earnings accumulate in your equity accounts. That contributes to the financial strength your business needs to justify bank loans. The lack of earnings erodes your firm's financial strength. So, we can say that a business must generate enough earnings to remain credit worthy.

As a practical matter, your business should show profitable operating results over several successive operating periods. A longer history of operating profitably always makes it easier to obtain a bank loan. That holds true even if a firm shows losses in its most recent operating period.

From another perspective, it becomes difficult to justify a bank loan to a business with persistent losses. Bankers cannot rely on projections that promise profits when a business has a history of continuing losses.

Bankers understand temporary financial setbacks. So, an occasional loss does not necessarily exclude your business from bank loans, but you must show the forces that set the stage for a return to profitable operations.

Chapter 8

Non-Financial Credit Criteria

Your firm's financial affairs remain the central concern in any bank credit decision, but bankers also review other factors that can become influential in the credit decision process. This chapter reviews the more prominent considerations.

Experience

In any circumstance, a banker's review of a request for a bank loan includes a look at the firm's past credit history with the bank. You want to show a history of managing your bank loans properly. That will appear obvious to most managers. The failure to repay past loans naturally disqualifies a business from new loans. But, handling a bank's loan properly also requires more than the eventual repayment of a loan.

> **Bank Note No. 14:**
> A firm's credit history with its bank influences its potential for receiving loans in the future.

Bankers expect borrowers to make interest and principal payments as scheduled. Yet, many business managers ignore those schedules. They make payments erratically. They appear on a bank's past due lists.

Repaying a loan does not erase a bank's records of a firm's slow payment habits. A record of slow payments can disqualify a business from a new bank loan. Moreover, that can occur even if your firm's financial affairs mark it as a credit worthy enterprise.

Trade Credit History

Suppliers still provide the bulk of the short-term financing available to businesses. So, paying your trade creditors promptly remains important for an independent business. A prompt payment record is essential in order to maintain that source of financing as a business grows. Your trade credit history also influences its chances of receiving bank credit consideration.

> **Bank Note No. 15:**
> Bankers expect borrowers to
> manage trade credit properly.

A history of prompt payments to suppliers improves your prospects for a bank loan. A history of slow payments has the opposite effect. Trade payment habits might not appear relevant in a decision about a bank loan. A manager may honor bank debts while not paying all suppliers as agreed. But bankers view prompt trade payment habits as a sign of good management. A business that pays its suppliers promptly continues to receive trade credit consideration. Those who pay slowly can find that consideration in jeopardy. Also, paying suppliers promptly proves concern about honoring a firm's credit obligations in a timely manner. That concern also applies to bank credit consideration.

On the other hand, a bank loan often produces the cash a business needs to achieve a prompt payment record. That realization tempers a banker's view of a recent history of slow trade credit payments.

But again, anticipating those needs before your payables fall past due provides another indication of the prudent management that helps justify a bank loan. A reputation as a slow payer in the trade registers the opposite effect.

Note that a prudent banker will independently verify your trade credit history. Most often, the verification comes from local trade credit associations. However, in some circumstances, banks do direct checks with a firm's prominent suppliers.

Some borrowers object to these checks. However, the validity inherent in the information that results makes them necessary. That also makes your firm's trade credit history a valid consideration in the credit decision process.

Management Ability

Good managers develop creative strategies to achieve business success. Good managers also come up with creative solutions to the unforeseen problems that can arise in a business. That creativity can increase the potential for the success of an independent business enterprise. Strong management ability can tip the scale in favor of a loan. Weak management can become an obstacle to the bank's approval of a loan request.

> **Bank Note No. 16:**
> Management ability remains
> the most important element
> in a bank's credit analysis.

Many will find those facts surprising. Many considerations included in the estimate of management ability elude direct measure. Much of the estimate rests on opinion. However, bankers work with many managers in many circumstances. Although businesses differ, the elements that represent good management remain common to most.

Good managers usually have good communication skills. They recognize their own strengths and weaknesses. They understand the strengths and weaknesses of their employees. They also show a sound knowledge of the more important aspects of the environment affecting their firms.

Good managers also exhibit good character. They operate honestly and ethically in all business circumstances. The lack of character can disqualify a business from a bank loan.

The experience bankers gain from working with many managers builds the foundation for evaluating management character and ability. Good managers stand out—so do those who fall short. Although errors occur, experienced bankers can typically make the distinction between the two.

Economic Conditions

Current local and national economic conditions remain an important consideration in any bank's credit decision process. You can easily predict how economic conditions can influence a bank's credit decisions.

> **Bank Note No. 17:**
> A strong economy makes approval
> of a bank loan more likely.

A strong economy increases the likelihood that well managed businesses will prosper. Also, an expanding economy can spur a marginal operation into a profitable operation. Those circumstances reduce the risk a bank incurs from making a loan.

A weak economy damages the sales and profits of almost every business enterprise. So, general economic malaise becomes an obstacle to the success of every business enterprise. That includes businesses that enjoy significant promise. Bankers become more conservative during such periods.

The same logic extends to local economic conditions. A strong national economy cannot offset the negative effects from a decline in particular industries. The local damage caused by declines exhibited in steel, copper, and other basic industries in towns historically dominated by these firms cannot be offset by an otherwise strong national economy.

Who Makes the Credit Decision

Most banks and bankers use the basic criteria discussed here to orient the credit decision process. However, the particular process that leads to a credit decision varies among banks. Some banks use systems that allow individual lending officers to make credit decisions. Within limits, each officer has the authority to approve or decline a request for a business loan. When the size of a loan request exceeds an officer's limit, the officer must seek approval from a more senior officer with a higher credit authority.

Other banks use a team approach to make credit decisions. That approach requires two or more lending officers to approve a firm's request for a loan. The makeup of any team will vary with the size of the loan. More senior lending officers participate in decisions involving large loans.

As another alternative, some banks use committees to make major credit decisions. In such instances, individual officers typically retain some lending authority, but loan requests above individual limits require the approval of the appropriate credit committee.

In more recent years, credit scoring processes have replaced the individual or credit committee decision process. This process is discussed in chapter 12.

As a practical matter, the decision structure in a bank should not stand as a prominent concern, but you should recognize the structure that exists in your bank. That can contribute to the communication process between you and your banker.

Differences among Banks

The criteria discussed in this chapter reflect general guidelines that orient the credit decisions in most banks. However, many loans declined by some banks will be approved by others.

Moreover, the approvals will result from prudent bankers exercising sound credit judgment. The differences stem from several premises. However, the focus here centers on those that are more prominent.

Bank Note No. 18:
Some banks approve loans
that others decline.

First, experience counts. Banks with significant experience in an industry feel comfortable with loans that other banks decline. For example, some banks gain extensive experience making loans secured by aircraft. Other banks rarely see a request for a loan secured by a personal or corporate airplane. The first set of banks become more likely to approve a loan to help a customer buy an airplane.

As another example, a bank located in an industrial district gains experience making loans secured by industrial machinery and equipment. A suburban bank located in the same city will lack that experience, so they will tend to shy away from such loans.

Experience with a particular customer can also influence a bank's loan decision. A loan request that fails to meet a bank's standard criteria can become acceptable because of the customer's reputation and past performance. Another bank that lacks that experience may decline a similar request from the same customer.

From another perspective, a bank's previous unfortunate experience with a particular business or industry can also become an influence in the credit decision process. A bank that has sustained a bad debt write-off resulting from a loan to a furniture store will shy away from similar loan requests. That often holds true even if the latter request comes from a borrower that satisfies the bank's normal credit criteria.

As a result of the complexities involved, some banks purposely develop expertise in specific types of loans. For example, some banks gain expertise making loans secured by accounts receivable and inventory. That enables them to make such loans comfortably. Other banks without that expertise will decline the same loans.

Different perspectives of their obligations of community service can also lead to different credit decisions by banks. One bank may approve a loan that fails to meet its normal criteria because of the potential contribution a firm's success will have on the local economy. Another bank may ignore that potential as an influence in the credit decision process.

The differences among banks does not imply any criticism of any banks or bankers. Experience and perspective play important roles in many business decisions, so it stands to reason that that these factors would also figure into any loan decision made by a banker.

Chapter 9

Collateral and Bank Credit Consideration

Banks often expect borrowers to pledge collateral to secure a loan, i.e., some business assets. That holds true even if a bank's analysis marks a business as a credit worthy operation. This chapter reviews the rationale behind that requirement.

Why Banks Require Collateral

Banks often expect borrowers to pledge collateral as security for a loan. However, collateral seldom stands as the deciding factor in a bank's credit decision.

From a banker's perspective, pledging a firm's assets cannot transform a questionable credit risk into a good loan. So, a banker's request for collateral to secure a loan does not necessarily imply any doubt about a borrower's basic credit worthiness.

> **Bank Note No. 19:**
> Collateral gives a bank an
> extra measure of protection.

A prudent lender expects a firm's operations to produce the funds necessary to repay a loan. The funds to repay a single payment loan presumably come from the source identified at the time the bank makes the loan. Alternatively, the cash flow that develops in the normal course of its operations provides the funds a business uses to repay an installment or revolving loan.

Of course, any projected primary source of repayment extends into an uncertain future. The primary source of repayment may fail to develop or fall short. Recognizing that potential, banks look for a secondary source of repayment to back up the primary source. Should a severe problem leave a business incapable of repaying a loan, the bank can sell the collateral to get the funds necessary for payment.

Business Assets That Serve as Collateral

Any business asset can serve as collateral for a bank loan. Of course, that excludes collateral already pledged to secure other loans. But, not all of a firm's assets have equal collateral value.

> **Bank Note No. 20:**
> Bankers view accounts receivable
> as more desirable collateral
> for a business loan.

A firm's accounts receivables represent customers' promises to pay for completed sales. So, they stand as liquid assets that customer payments will soon convert into cash within a predictable period. That provides banks with the largest measure of collateral security typically available from an independent business.

> **Bank Note No. 21:**
> Inventory is less desirable
> collateral for a bank loan.

Inventory can also be used for collateral, though bankers view this as a less desirable form. That surprises many business managers who invest in the stock that represents the focal point of the firm's operations. Yet, several factors make inventory less desirable collateral for a loan than a firm's accounts receivables.

First, receivables represent the proceeds from completed sales. Presuming the products or services arrive as agreed, each buyer has an obligation to pay for the purchases. That gives the business a legal claim on a cash payment. A bank that takes receivables as collateral can also enforce that right to repay a loan.

In contrast, a sale stands as a prerequisite to convert inventory into cash. Although that appears obvious, a banker has to measure the collateral value of inventory using its potential liquidation value if a business fails. Experience proves that the value of a firm's inventory drops significantly when a bank attempts to sell it as part of its effort to liquidate a loan.

Another circumstance also reduces the collateral value of a firm's inventory. A business contending with financial difficulties will sell most of its inventory. That is a natural step to try to survive.

Sales eliminate a firm's best stock long before a banker makes the decision to take the inventory that serves as collateral for a loan. That makes inventory less valuable to a bank as collateral than it is to a business, which views it as potential sales.

Lastly, a bank has more difficulty keeping track of the collateral value that a firm's inventory represents. Banks can easily keep track of the changes in the collateral value of a firm's accounts receivable. A bank can use invoices and customer payments to record changes in the value of those receivables. Evidence of the changes in the value of a firm's inventory is often more difficult to document.

In any event, a bank seldom takes inventory as collateral without also taking a pledge of a firm's accounts receivable. A firm's receivables represent the proceeds from the sale of its inventory. Separating the two assets in any collateral pledge is illogical.

Similarly, a bank that takes accounts receivable as the primary collateral for a business loan typically adds the firm's inventory as additional collateral. The logic noted above also explains that action. Although exceptions exist, separating the two assets in any collateral pledge seldom makes sense.

Banks will assign a high collateral value to machinery and equipment commonly used by several businesses. Lathes, fork lifts, and standard delivery vehicles stand as common examples. Such equipment usually remains easily salable should a borrower meet financial difficulty.

In contrast to inventory, the fixed assets used in a firm's operations usually remain a necessity. So, they remain in place when a business confronts financial difficulties. A lender has less concern about any erosion in the value of the machinery and equipment taken as collateral for a loan.

However, banks will usually assign a lower collateral value to specialized machinery and equipment. For example, the equipment used to manufacture decorative pottery cannot be easily adapted to any other purpose. That limits the collateral value of the equipment used in the pottery manufacturing process.

The distinction between equipment with high and low collateral value often becomes a point of dispute between business managers and bankers. Business managers focus on the value of the machinery and equipment used in their businesses as going concerns. They seldom consider business failure as possible outcome.

However, bankers see many businesses in many circumstances. As an indisputable fact, many businesses fail. So, bankers have to make the above distinctions when assigning collateral value to the machinery and equipment businesses pledge as collateral for bank loans. The market value of specialized equipment diminishes severely when a bank tries to sell it during the liquidation process.

Collateral Advance Rates

A collateral pledge by a business does not transform a questionable credit into a good loan. Collateral makes a good loan better. But, collateral can exert another influence on the credit consideration a bank extends to a business—that influence is on the size of the loan. This occurs when a bank sets the amount of a loan as a percentage of the assets pledged as collateral.

> **Bank Note No. 23:**
> Collateral can influence the size
> of the loan a bank makes to a business.

Many considerations affect the amount a bank will advance against any collateral a business pledges. However, you can use the following advance rates as general guidelines for your expectations:

Collateral	Advance Rate	Normal Loan Limit Per $10,000 in Collateral Value
Accounts Receivable	50–80%	$5,000–8,000
Inventory	20–50%	$2,000–5,000
Machinery and equipment	50–80%	$5,000–7,500

So, a business with $10,000 in bona fide accounts receivable can expect a $5,000 to $8,000 loan secured by those receivables. More credit worthy borrowers will qualify for a loan approaching the upper end of that range. A less credit worthy business will find its advance rate set near or below the lower end of the range. The same factors also influence the advance rates applicable to the other business collateral included in the schedule.

As already noted, many interrelated factors influence the advance rate a bank approves against any collateral a business may pledge to secure a loan. However, apart from a firm's financial condition, the requirements a bank sets to monitor the value of the pledged collateral stand most prominently.

The Collateral Monitoring Processes

A bank often asks for a collateral pledge merely as a precautionary measure of extra security for a good loan. In most cases, other than the legal documents necessary to secure the collateral pledge, the question of collateral does not arise again either for the bank or the business. The pledge remains legally valid, but it stands as a formality.

In other instances, a bank asks for collateral to provide tangible support for its credit consideration. In those instances, banks often include reporting requirements to help insure that enough collateral exists to secure the bank's loan.

Again, no standard reporting requirements exist. The requirements vary with the bank and the borrower's circumstances. However, reporting requirements typically increase for larger loans. More stringent reporting requirements also tend to accompany loans to financially weaker borrowers.

In any instance, collateral reporting requirements seldom become onerous as long as the business manager readily responds to the banker's requests. Meeting those requirements makes a banker more comfortable with the lending relationship.

> **Bank Note No. 24:**
> A business manager should respond readily
> to a banker's request to carry out
> collateral reporting requirements.

Pledging Personal Assets to Secure a Business Loan

On occasion, pledging business assets may not provide the boost that a firm needs to qualify for a loan. The collateral may not be enough to overcome negative aspects of a firm's financial circumstances. Or, the collateral may simply be inadequate to compensate for a firm's weak financial characteristics. When this happens, the business owner or a major stockholder may be asked to pledge personal assets as collateral.

Bank Note No. 25:
A stockholder can pledge personal assets
to secure a bank loan to a business.

Pledging personal certificates of deposit, common stocks, or equity in real estate can compensate for circumstances that otherwise disqualify a business from a bank loan. Of course, before pledging any personal assets to secure a business loan, you should try to estimate the potential success of your enterprise as objectively as possible. That should include consideration of opinions from respected friends and business associates.

Pledging personal assets in those instances represents a serious risk for the owner. But, pledging personal assets can make sense when a bank loan can provide the financial aid that enables a marginal operation to become profitable.

Naturally, separating the two sets of circumstances remains a difficult task. Undue optimism can easily obscure financial facts that suggest dim prospects for a firm's future. On the other hand, sometimes a business owner's optimism and personal drive can transform dim prospects into business success. Unfortunately, no formula exists for distinguishing between the two sets of circumstances.

Small Business Administration Loans

Many promising businesses do not qualify for standard bank credit consideration. Some lack the financial strength necessary to justify a loan. Others lack a profitable operating history. Some others do not have enough collateral to secure a bank loan. In such instances, a business may find a loan involving the Small Business Administration (SBA) as an alternative form of financing.

> **Bank Note No. 26:**
> An SBA loan can be a beneficial
> form of business financing.

Unfortunately, some borrowers remain unaware of the SBA loan alternative. Others shy away from SBA loans because of imaginary mounds of paperwork and an unrealistic fear of government intervention.

This chapter dispels the misconceptions that many business managers have about SBA loans. You will find an easy application process and little prospect of government intervention. Most importantly, you will find that SBA loans can help a struggling enterprise gain the financing necessary to fulfill its promise and become a profitable business venture.

Two Categories of Loans

Congress created the Small Business Administration as an independent federal agency in 1953. Under its Congressional mandate, the SBA operates several programs designed to benefit small business.

The concern here centers on the potential help a business can get from an SBA loan. The SBA's business loan program includes two major categories of loans:

1. Direct loans from funds Congress appropriates, and
2. Bank loans partially guarantied by the SBA.

We can dismiss discussion about direct loans from the SBA. In recent years, Congress has decreased its appropriations for direct loans. Continuing budgetary restrictions make elimination of the direct loan program likely. In any event, demand for direct loans far outstrips the supply. So, the discussion here centers on SBA loans originated by banks.

Most SBA Loans Come from Banks

Banks make most of the loans that stand as SBA loans, but these loans come with a partial guarantee against loss issued by the SBA. The guarantee now stands around 75 percent to 80 percent, depending upon the size of the loan. But on occasion, the SBA guaranties smaller proportions of some bank loans.

The SBA's proportionate guaranty remains fixed over the term of a loan. An 80 percent guaranty applies to any portion of the debt outstanding.

To illustrate, let's assume a bank makes a $100,000 loan partially backed by an SBA guaranty for 80 percent of the loan. On the day the bank makes the loan, the SBA's financial risk from non-payment totals $80,000. The bank incurs the other $20,000 in risk.

That fractional relationship holds constant as the borrower pays the loan. When repayments reduce the principal balance on the loan to $90,000, the SBA's risk of loss from its 80 percent guaranty drops to $81,000. The risk for the other $9,000 remains with the bank.

The same relationship remains throughout the loan's repayment period. The SBA has $8,000 in exposure when the borrower has repaid all but $10,000 on a guarantied loan. The bank's 20 percent exposure then becomes $2,000.

> **Bank Note No. 27:**
> The SBA can guarantee bank loans
> to a maximum of $750,000.

A $750,000 limit exists on the total dollar amount of a bank's loan the SBA can guarantee. That does not limit the size of the SBA guarantied loan a bank can make to a borrower, but the SBA cannot guarantee more than $750,000 out of any larger loan.

For example, a bank can make a $1 million SBA guarantied loan to a business. However, should the borrower default, the SBA can reimburse the bank for no more than $750,000 out of any loss that results.

The guaranty still reduces the bank's financial exposure, but many banks remain reluctant to make guarantied loans in amounts that exceed that covered by the SBA's $750,000 limit.

To preclude a misunderstanding, we should enter a note of caution. An SBA guaranty for a loan limits a bank's loss if a borrower defaults. However, that guaranty does not reduce the borrower's obligation to repay the loan in full.

When a borrower defaults, the SBA reimburses the bank for the uninsured portion of the loan. SBA representatives then turn to the task of collecting the loan from the business.

That becomes more significant when we recognize that every SBA loan to a business requires personal guaranties from the firm's principals. Should the liquidation of the firm's assets prove insufficient to repay the loan, the SBA looks to the guarantors to make up the shortage.

Eligibility for SBA Loans

SBA loans fill a void for independent businesses unable to obtain conventional loans from banks or other lenders. But, not every business is eligible for such loans. SBA loans are generally geared toward independent, profit seeking businesses.

Bank Note No. 28:
SBA loans remain restructured to independent,
profit seeking business enterprises.

That excludes larger businesses that have access to equity or borrowed funds from traditional sources. However, the term "small business" can be misleading. Many larger firms easily meet the standards that qualify a business for an SBA loan.

To illustrate, let's look at the current eligibility requirements for businesses:

Manufacturing

Maximum number of employees may range from 500 up to 1,500, depending on the industry in which the applicant is primarily engaged.

Wholesaling

Yearly sales must not be over $9.5 to $22 million, depending on the industry; maximum number of employees may not exceed 100.

Services

Annual receipts not exceeding $2.5million to $21.5 million, depending on the industry.

Retailing

Annual sales or receipts not exceeding $5 to $21 million, depending on the industry.

General Construction

Average annual receipts not exceeding $13.5 million to $17 million, depending on the industry.

Special Trade Construction

Average annual receipts not exceeding $7 million.

Agriculture

Annual receipts not exceeding .5 million to $9 million, depending on the industry.

The standards are subject to change. But, as they now stand, most independent enterprises can qualify as small businesses. It should, however, be noted that some industries are not eligible for SBA loans, e.g., publishing.

The Credit Requirements

An SBA loan stands as an option when a business does not qualify for a traditional bank loan. That means that the firm no longer has to satisfy the financial credit criteria discussed in chapter 7. But, a borrower still must satisfy some stringent credit criteria.

First, a borrower must have some equity capital at risk in the enterprise. A minimum of 30 percent to 50 percent of the total capital for the business must be provided by the owner. For a new business venture, that equity must come from an actual cash investment. An existing business can use its equity to substitute for all or part of the required cash investment.

> **Bank Note No. 29:**
> The owner(s) must provide
> 30 percent to 50 percent of
> the total capital for a business venture.

A borrower must also show that the firm's beginning or existing capital, coupled with the SBA loan, will enable the business to operate on a sound financial basis. In combination with the firm's capital, the SBA loan should enable the business to honor its normal credit obligations and operate profitably.

An applicant for an SBA loan must also show a reasonable probability that the firm can repay the loan. The evidence comes from the past earnings records and future prospects for an existing business. The evidence for a new business venture comes from logical projections that look at the expectations for the firm's first five years in operation.

A business must also secure an SBA loan with enough collateral to help assure repayment. The collateral may include personal assets pledged by the personal guarantors. The cumulative total value of the collateral pledged must be enough to compensate for potential errors in the estimates of a borrower's prospects for repayment.

As another logical requirement, a borrower must show the management ability necessary to operate the business successfully. Experience managing an existing enterprise can meet that need. Experience as an employee in a similar operation may also meet that requirement.

In some circumstances, showing management ability becomes more difficult. Borrowers seeking an SBA loan for new ventures often lack direct experience managing a business enterprise. But, a borrower must present the best evidence available.

Some of that evidence may come from a borrower's personal business experience. Educational background can also stand as evidence. Still more evidence can come as references from qualified individuals. The estimate of a borrower's ability to manage a new business successfully remains an imperfect, subjective process, but more reliable alternatives do not currently exist.

None of these credit standards insure that a borrower will repay an SBA loan in full. Projections extend into an uncertain future. Lenders inevitably make errors in their judgments of a borrower's prospects. Observing these basic credit standards leads to repayment of most bank guarantied SBA loans.

Two Myths about SBA Loans

Many managers view an SBA loan as a form of disaster financing. Banks presumably make SBA loans only to shift probable losses onto taxpayers, the real source of funding for the SBA.

The view that the SBA just bails banks out of bad loans represents an unfortunate myth. Errors undoubtedly occur, but the SBA will not provide a guaranty for a loan unless the borrower meets its credit standards.

> **Bank Note No. 30:**
> The SBA does not
> bail banks out of bad loans.

Inevitably, an extra note of caution enters any analysis of a proposed guarantied loan that includes repayment of an existing bank loan to a business. The SBA really has three options when the request for a loan guaranty includes the repayment of an existing bank loan.

As an obvious alternative, the SBA can refuse to guarantee a debt that absorbs part of an existing bad loan by a bank. SBA lending officers can usually separate sensible proposals from those really designed to salvage a bank from a bad position.

The SBA can also approve a proposed loan with a hybrid guaranty. The hybrid can exclude a bank's existing loans to a borrower but provide the SBA's guaranty for the larger portion of the new funds advanced to a business.

For example, assume a bank requests an SBA guaranty for a $150,000 loan to a struggling business. But, $50,000 of that total will replace an existing $50,000 debt the business owes to the bank. The other $100,000 represents new funds that can provide the financial fuel necessary for the borrower's success.

In this instance, the SBA can approve the loan with a guaranty that excludes the bank's existing $50,000 loan. An 85 percent guaranty then insures the repayment of $85,000. The burden for the old debt of $50,000 plus 15 percent, or $15,000, of the new funds advanced to the borrower still lies with the bank, should the business fail.

A hybrid loan really serves two logical objectives. First, the hybrid reduces the incentive unethical bankers would have to try to obtain an SBA guaranty for a bad loan. The SBA can still provide a guaranty when warranted and decline those loans where it obviously is not.

When the decision appears less obvious, the SBA can still help with a guaranty for the bulk of the new funds. The bank then retains the full exposure for the firm's existing debt obligation.

From a positive perspective, the hybrid guaranty enables the SBA to help a struggling business succeed. The SBA can help the business obtain new funds without the burden of absorbing a bank's existing risk. That benefits both the business and the bank.

However, it does not reduce the bank's risk. The bank's risk increases through its exposure on the new funds advanced in the SBA guaranteed loan. That encourages the bank to recommend only those hybrid loans that really have the potential to contribute to a firm's recovery.

As a final alternative, the SBA can guarantee a loan that replaces part of a firm's existing debt obligation to a bank. On occasion, the SBA does provide a guaranty in such circumstances, usually when the borrower shows a high probability for success.

Another myth associated with SBA guaranteed loans is that they are low risk ventures that banks presumably can make with little concern. After all, an SBA guaranty reduces a bank's potential loss to as little as 15 percent of a loan. Presumably, that should eliminate a bank's concern about the risk of repayment. This is not true.

> **Bank Note No. 31:**
> Banks do not make bad loans merely because of the SBA's partial guaranty for repayment.

As noted above, the SBA does not provide loan guaranties haphazardly. A borrower must first satisfy the SBA's credit standards. Failure to meet those standards precludes a guaranty, although a bank approves the loan. A bank's approval does not make the SBA guaranty automatic.

Moreover, the bank's share of the loss from a guaranteed loan that becomes uncollectible remains significant. At first glance, writing off only 15 percent of a guaranteed loan may seem a nominal consideration for a bank. However, that consideration becomes more significant when we remember that banks average only a 1 percent net return from their assets. So, absorbing $10,000 out of a $100,000 SBA guaranteed loan still stands as a significant loss. That write-off wipes out the net return from another $1,000,000 in good loans. This orientation encourages banks to exercise thoughtful lending practices, even when an SBA guaranty exists.

The Application Process

The application process for an SBA loan is simpler than many business managers imagine. Most borrowers enjoy immediate access to the information necessary for the application. The process then centers on completing the standard application forms and providing any supplemental information necessary for the lender's credit decision process.

Different circumstances among borrowers may change the information necessary for the application. For example, a loan request for a new business venture naturally lacks historical financial information. Recognizing that fact, let's review the essential information required for a new venture.

The essential information that should accompany a typical SBA loan application for an existing business includes:

1. The fiscal year-end income statements and balance sheets for the business.
2. A current balance sheet and income statement (less than sixty days old), if not satisfied by #1.
3. Three previous year's personal tax returns plus a current personal statement of financial position for all guarantors.
4. A proposal letter that summarizes the purpose and amount of the loan requested.
5. A brief history of the company.
6. Personal resumes on all management personnel.
7. A list of all collateral offered, accompanied by appraisals on estimated values.
8. A list of items that will be funded with the loan proceeds (which naturally become additional collateral for the loan), e.g., equipment, machinery, inventory.

Some managers will find these information requirements excessive. However, the information that pertains directly to the business is necessary for effective management in any circumstance. Every business needs current financial information; every business manager should have a sensible plan for distributing any borrowed funds; and every manager should feel comfortable reviewing and revealing the company's history and the personal experience of the major management personnel.

Borrowers may feel less comfortable revealing their personal financial circumstances, but a lender relying on a personal guaranty needs a look at the guarantor's ability to back up the firm's repayment capabilities. That ability can become the difference between the approval or disapproval of an SBA loan.

Some borrowers also remain reluctant to provide the required tax returns. That reluctance usually stems from past, arbitrary actions designed to reduce reported income tax obligations. Without making judgments about such actions, a business manager should recognize that the refusal to supply a firm's past tax returns can disqualify a business from an SBA loan.

After collecting the relevant items included in the above list, a borrower must also complete the standard SBA application forms. This task is simplified if the above information is already collected. Completing the SBA application is a straightforward process.

Submitting the completed forms and supporting information usually represents the final step in the application. The bank's declination naturally ends the application for an SBA guaranteed loan. You can then submit the application to another bank. As noted previously, banks differ. One bank may approve a loan that others decline.

If the bank approves the application for a guaranteed loan and the SBA's commitment follows, you then must fulfill any conditions that the bank or the SBA place as requirements prior to funding the loan.

After Loan Approval

The application process does not complete the paperwork associated with an SBA loan. Once approved, you must execute the promissory notes and other documents normally associated with any loan. That includes the personal guaranties from the principals in the business.

The SBA or lending banks often set specific requirements a borrower must fulfill before receiving any loan proceeds. Some requirements insure that the borrower initiates operations properly. Others help insure that the borrower uses the loan proceeds as intended. Some others represent extra caution that help protect the lender's position.

Specific requirements naturally vary among different borrowers, but the following list includes the more common requirements that accompany the conditional approval of SBA loans.

Before disbursement of any loan funds, lenders may require:

1. A copy of the executed lease on the borrower's business premise for the full term of the SBA loan; the lease may include options for renewal as part of the lease form.
2. Assignment of the lease with the right of reassignment.
3. Actual life insurance policy on the principal for the required amount; the policy must name the lender as beneficiary.
4. All necessary hazard insurance coverage.
5. Evidence of any cash injection required by the lender.
6. Articles of Incorporation (filed copy).
7. Employer's identification number issued by the IRS.
8. Copies of invoices or receipts for loan funds disbursed to buy equipment, fixtures, inventory, or other business assets.
9. Copy of Franchise Agreement.
10. Executed copy of a bill of sale.
11. Set of complete plans and specifications for construction purposes.
12. Builder's risk insurance.
13. Firm cost proposal from general contractor.

Again, recognize that these are only examples of common requirements that may accompany the approval of SBA loans. The specific requirements will naturally vary with each borrower's circumstances. Few loans will have a list as extensive as the one above.

Remember that lenders can also set additional requirements applicable to each borrower's unique circumstances. Any special requirements serve the same motives as the more common examples listed above.

Also, recognize that similar conditional requirements often accompany conventional bank loans. Borrowers usually meet those conditions with little concern. However, when part of the SBA loan process, these same requirements add to mythical mountains of paperwork imagined by many business managers. An SBA loan does involve paperwork. However, most of it is in the application process itself. The mountain of paperwork is only a myth.

The "Big Brother" Myth

Another myth commonly associated with SBA loans also deserves some attention. That myth says that any business that obtains an SBA loan automatically invites the federal government into its operations. In its most extreme form, the myth makes the federal government the borrower's managing partner.

An SBA loan does not invite government intervention into a firm's operation. The SBA lacks both the incentive and the resources to become involved in the operation of thousands of borrowers spread across the country. After obtaining the loan, a borrower's concern with the SBA usually remains limited to making the monthly payment.

Of course, if your business fails, the SBA becomes involved in the liquidation process. Any other lender will have the same response. A lender's direct involvement in the liquidation process increases the prospects for eventual repayment of its loan.

The Benefits of an SBA Loan

SBA loans obviously benefit businesses unable to qualify for conventional bank financing. Apart from that, SBA loans have features that can make them attractive to businesses that qualify for standard bank loans.

The repayment terms for an SBA loan stand as the most attractive feature. Banks typically do not extend commercial loans with repayment terms that extend beyond four or five years. Moreover, even when making such loans, banks often make the loans come due each year so they can review a firm's credit worthiness annually.

That can lead to unforeseen changes in the repayment schedule for a loan. For example, a bank may elect to shorten the repayment from a five-year term to a two- or three-year term. Such a change can have a significant, detrimental effect on a firm's cash flow.

In contrast, an SBA loan usually extends from five to seven years. On occasion, SBA loans even can extend out to ten years or longer. Moreover, an SBA loan has a fixed amortization schedule.

Presuming the business operates successfully, the repayment schedule does not change.

Table 10-1 illustrates the potential benefit from the longer terms available from an SBA loan. A $100,000 SBA loan at a 9 percent annual interest rate over seven years leaves a business with a $1,609 monthly payment. That falls significantly below the $3,179 monthly payment required to repay a $100,000 bank loan over three years. This payment requirement can make the SBA loan more attractive, even if the business qualifies for conventional bank credit consideration.

An SBA loan can also help a business obtain a larger loan than a bank can offer on conventional terms. A business that qualifies for a $100,000 conventional bank loan may qualify for a $200,000 loan supported by a partial guaranty from the SBA. That can become a significant benefit for a business with ambitious plans.

Table 10-1: Monthly Payments for $100,000 Loan at a 9 Percent Annual Percentage Rate

Repayment Period (yrs.)	Monthly Payment
1	$8,945
2	$4,569
3	$3,180
4	$2,488
5	$2,076
6	$1,803
7	$1,609
8	$1,465
9	$1,354
10	$1,260

Despite its fixed amortization schedule, an SBA loan leaves you with a surprising degree of flexibility to contend with an uncertain future.

If you encounter unforeseen problems, the SBA will often allow your business to defer principal repayments for several months. That can provide the financial relief necessary to overcome your problems.

Of course, from a positive perspective, your operating performance might far exceed original expectations. That success can raise the need for additional funds to continue the growth. In such instances, the SBA will often release part of its collateral liens to help your business obtain new funds to fuel more growth.

Moreover, those releases may leave the original amortization schedule for the SBA loan intact. You may gain the extended repayment schedule for the SBA loan and still gain the ability to obtain new funds.

Banks also benefit from SBA guarantied loans. Partial repayment guaranties help justify many loans that otherwise would become declining loans. That adds to the interest earnings that represent the primary source of income for a bank.

Over the longer term, banks also benefit when SBA loans help small, struggling enterprises grow into large, profitable businesses. SBA loans often set the foundation for a strong, mutually profitable financial partnership between a business and a bank.

What Makes Bankers Conservative?

Many business managers view commercial bank loan officers as cautious, conservative lenders who are unwilling to take risks. That conservatism is sometimes viewed as an effort to prevent banks from providing the financial aid struggling businesses need to grow and prosper. But, the conservatism apparent among commercial bank lenders stems from a simple arithmetic fact.

Banks have a very small profit margin. Using the common industry measure, the average bank earns only a 1 percent return from its assets. That 1 percent return translates into only $10,000 in earnings annually from each $1 million in assets a bank owns.

Loans remain the largest proportion of a bank's earning assets. They provide the bulk of the typical bank's income. But, loans that become uncollectible also pose the greatest threat to that income. Such loans force prudent bankers to become conservative lenders.

A look at two views of the effects loan losses have on a bank's earnings lends support to that claim.

Two Views of a Bank's Loan Losses

The first view centers on the earnings a bank realizes from $10 million in loans. A 1 percent return on assets results in only $100,000 in earnings from that loan portfolio.

That means that a bank that cannot collect a $100,000 bad loan must have $10 million in good loans outstanding for a full year to off-set the loss. Practical financial necessity makes prudent banker's conservative. They enjoy little margin for error.

The second view of the damage from loan losses again centers on the $10 million loan portfolio noted above. Now, we assume that the portfolio includes one hundred loans for $100,000 each.

We find that a lender responsible for those loans needs remarkable foresight. Making one incorrect decision that leads to one uncollectible $100,000 loan erases the earnings expected from the full $10 million loan portfolio. An incorrect lending decision one out of a hundred times erases the profit from ninety-nine correct decisions.

The problem becomes more severe when we recognize that nine out of ten business ventures end in failure. That failure rate creates a difficult dilemma for commercial bank lenders.

Commercial bank lenders have a slim margin of error; to operate profitably, they must make correct loan decisions more than 99 percent of the time. Since 90 percent of all independent business ventures fail, a conservative approach to lending becomes the only logical way to resolve the dilemma.

Despite the slim margin for error, banks continue to make loans to businesses. Most banks continue to operate profitably. So, we should see how bankers compensate for the small margin of error inherent in the lending process.

How Banks Try to Prevent Loan Losses

First, banks restrict most of their loans to existing businesses with a history of profitable operations. Past profits provide the basis for expecting profits in the future. That expectation helps justify a positive response to a request for a bank loan.

In contrast, new business ventures lack an operating history. The high business failure rate creates a logical obstacle to any bank loan. Lacking other considerations, the low margin of error lenders usually have makes that obstacle insurmountable.

Logically, producing profits over several successive operating periods increases a firm's chances for a bank loan. One profitable quarter following two years of losses stands as an anomaly. But, generating profits over ten successive quarters creates a track record that supports expectations about the firm's continuing success.

From another perspective, prudent bank lenders also understand that occasional losses can temporarily interrupt a successful firm's profitable operations.

Temporary losses may result from unexpected supplier price hikes, labor disputes, or any number of company-specific problems. Loss may also come from the temporary drop in sales associated with a general economic slowdown.

When such losses occur, a lender will ask for an explanation. The lender needs to understand why the loss occurred and needs to see the firm's plans for a return to profitable operations. That information provides the premise for continuing the bank's credit consideration.

Bankers are conservative, but they are also in touch with business reality. They know that even successful businesses can experience temporary setbacks.

In any event, restricting loans to profitable firms does not compensate for the small margin of error that confronts bankers. So, bankers take other steps to help increase the chances for the eventual repayment of its loans to business borrowers.

Other Steps to Reduce Bank Loan Losses

Bankers usually take collateral pledges to support a business loan. A business typically must pledge its accounts receivable, inventory, machinery and equipment, or other assets to secure a bank loan. If a business fails to repay the loan, the bank can liquidate the collateral necessary to repay the bank's credit consideration.

As a practical matter, requiring collateral to secure a business loan really serves another purpose. No banker wants to liquidate a firm's operating assets to pay off a bank loan. Exercising that option obviously means the end of the business. Instead, that potential provides bankers with a valuable psychological lever. Borrowers become more attentive to their bank debt obligations when the firm's assets remain at risk. That attention increases the probability for the eventual repayment of the bank's loan.

When making larger loans, banks often gain additional leverage by using loan agreements to govern the credit relationship. A loan agreement imposes financial and operating constraints on a borrower designed to maintain the firm's credit worthiness. Violating any constraint represents a default that allows the bank to demand immediate repayment of the loan. Chapter 15 discusses the more common requirements that appear in loan agreements.

As another step to reduce risk, bankers usually expect a firm's principal owners to guarantee any bank loans to the business. That requirement proceeds from some logical premises.

First, bankers want to prevent shareholders from draining loan proceeds from the business for their personal uses. Making the principals personally liable for the firm's bank debt obligations provides a measure of protection against that potential problem.

A second premise for requiring a personal guaranty stems from a need to maintain the principal's interest if the business encounters financial difficulties.

That premise may come as a surprise. Working through business difficulties seems to stand as a logical management objective, but that presumption ignores a critical fact. Financial pressure from the need to pay suppliers, meet payroll, and honor tax obligations can become a frustrating burden for the most conscientious manager. That frustration can make some business managers abandon the effort necessary to solve the firm's problems. A personal guaranty ensures the lender that the problems will not just be abandoned.

A firm's failure to repay its bank loans poses a threat to the guarantor's personal financial circumstances. That encourages a prudent guarantor to turn the frustration into a challenge. Meeting the challenge solves the problem for both the bank and the borrower. That also reduces the risk that accompanies a bank's loan to a business.

The Balance Bankers Walk

Banks add financial fuel to the economy by making business loans. So, the credit criteria discussed above will appear too conservative to many managers. Using such restrictive credit criteria seem to set obstacles that make their mission more difficult to achieve.

However, banks are not public, non-profit institutions dedicated to improving the economy. They operate as profit seeking businesses with a responsibility to generate a profit for their shareholders. Those shareholders will replace any management group that fails to produce a satisfactory level of earnings.

> **Bank Note No. 32:**
> Conservative lending practices stand
> as a necessity for a bank's profitability.

Making sure that loans are only granted to responsible businesses who will repay their obligation in a timely manner is a necessity for a profitable bank. The average bank earns only a 1 percent return on its assets. That tiny margin leaves little room for errors in the lending decision process.

Credit Scoring Principles

The discussion regarding how banks review business loan requests is valid. The credit criteria is valid from a banker's perspective and also continues to set parameters that help orient independent business financial management.

However, the wave of mergers among banks, coupled with the desire to operate more efficiently, has altered the credit decision process. Most large banks now make many business decisions using credit scoring decision criteria.

The same criteria discussed previously in this section orient that scoring process. That is, the same financial criteria enter into the scoring process, along with additional criteria.

Of course, the specific credit scoring model will vary among banks. No industry-wide model exists. However, a general perspective that underlies the commercial credit scoring model will help you understand the process.

Logically, a credit scoring model proceeds from a statistical model drawn from a bank's historical experience with a large number of borrowers. Based on the statistical history among past borrowers, a bank identifies the criteria that separates those loans that paid as agreed from those that eventually became uncollectible, bad debt receivables.

The size of loans subject to credit scoring will vary among banks. Some banks will use credit scoring for business loans up to $50,000. Others will use credit scoring for loans up to $500,000.

The credit scoring process involves some straightforward logic. A bank identifies the parameters (discussed below) that distinguish a sound credit risk from a questionable risk. That is, how likely the borrower is to pay a loan versus how likely the borrower will default.

So, when subject to credit scoring, your business gets the loan if the parameters score sufficient points that match or exceed the positive decision criterion. If your credit fails to gather the necessary points, the bank denies your loan request.

In many instances, banks make the credit scoring process invisible to their customers. That is, the customers are not aware that a bank's business loan decisions proceed from a credit scoring process instead of an individual's judgment. Knowledge that the credit scoring process, rather than an individual, is making the decisions would make some borrowers feel "depersonalized."

However, if curiosity prevails, simply ask your banker if the bank uses credit scoring for the credit decision process. Your knowledge will not alter the system, but you may want to switch banks if you want to have personal judgments govern the process.

The Premise for Credit Scoring

As a practical matter, the option for locating a bank that does not use credit scoring for small business loans will continue to diminish in the future. That stems from a logical focus on the profitability that comes from operating more efficiently. Analysis shows that approximately 10 percent of a typical bank's business loans of $100,000 or less required nearly 64 percent of the commercial loan department's time. That time commitment forces (or will force) banks to use credit scoring to compete effectively.

However, credit scoring can also become advantageous for business owners. The credit scoring process often reduces the requirement for all the business and personal financial documentation required for the traditional judgmental analysis by loan officers. Moreover, the credit scoring process returns decisions more rapidly. The process operates more efficiently for the bank and the borrower.

However, note that a disqualification of a loan request based on a credit scoring statistical model is not necessarily the final decision on the matter. In some instances, an "override" might counter the denial of the loan by the credit scoring system.

The "override" might stem from a longstanding relationship with the bank or particular banker. A history of satisfactory performance in repaying previous loans also makes a logical contribution to a bank overriding a loan disqualified by the credit scoring system.

The Elements in a Credit Scoring System

Any credit scoring system comes from a statistical model. The model provides a rank order view of the risks associated with different borrowers. Logical considerations enter into the development of a credit scoring model.

One primary criterion comes from the borrower's historical payment experience on previous loans extended by the bank to the borrower. The model will look at three aspects of the borrower's payment history.

First, the model will measure the frequency of a borrowers past due payments. Logically, the more frequently a customer was delinquent, the more the credit scoring model penalizes the borrower.

Another consideration centers on the recovery of a borrower's delinquent payments. Perhaps a borrower has a history of prompt payments, but more recent records show apparent deterioration in the firm's prompt payment habits. The deterioration raises a warning sign that reduces the positive points a firm receives in the credit scoring process.

As another logical consideration, the more serious the delinquency, the more damage the delinquency does to the firm's chance of obtaining a bank loan. A recent loan payment that went over ninety days past due almost guarantees denial of a loan request.

Note that payment histories of both the business and the business owner enter into the credit scoring process. A history of lax payment habits in either instance then becomes an obstacle to accumulating the points necessary to obtain a business loan.

The credit scoring process also considers a firm's payment history with its trade conditions. Again, some modest slow payments may not lend to the denial of a loan request. But, depending upon the particular credit scoring system, at least half of a firm's trade balances should reflect prompt payment histories.

Some matters of public record also enter into the credit scoring process. If your business has suffered a bankruptcy, any bank credit consideration becomes unlikely. In some instances, large national concerns can obtain bank loans immediately after going into Chapter 11 proceedings designed to reorganize and continue operations. Smaller businesses seldom have the same opportunity.

Bank credit consideration also becomes less likely if one or more liens or judgments have been filed against you or your business. Certainly, judgments can stem from honest business disagreements, but bankers typically view them negatively. So, liens or judgments lower your credit score.

Generic Considerations

Some factors influencing a credit score remain out of a firm's influence. For example, some credit scoring systems will include a look at the risk presumed inherent in the firm's industry. A business that manufactures chemicals will receive fewer points than a wholesale grocery distributor. The nature of the chemical manufacturer's operations mark it as a more risky operation than a grocery distributor.

That may seem an unfair distinction from a chemical manufacturer's perspective. Attentive management can reduce much of the risk associated with a chemical manufacturing process. However, few bankers come qualified to judge the safety associated with the production of chemicals. It is easier to understand the nature of a wholesale grocer's operation.

Scoring systems will typically distinguish the risk among various industries using codes that identify industry groups. The codes come from Standard Industry Classification (SIC) numbers that distinguish industry groups. The scoring systems then add or subtract points according to the risk perceived in a business that occupies a particular SIC group.

Financial Considerations

Chapter 7 reviews the financial credit criteria that oriented a banker's traditional perspective of a business loan request. Those criteria, i.e., a firm's liquidity, financial strength, and profitability, will also enter the credit scoring process.

Logically, better liquidity, financial strength, and profitability adds to the potential for a positive response to a business loan request. Signs of financial weakness in any area will result in a lower credit score.

Do not misunderstand. Some financial weakness, compared to industry standards, does not necessarily eliminate the prospects for a bank loan to a business, but it does affect the point total necessary to qualify for a bank loan.

Management Response

Some business managers will remain resistant to lenders who use credit scoring to respond to business loan requests. They will continue to prefer the personal judgment of a bank loan officer. They will continue the presumption that a personal relationship with a loan officer can tip a close loan decision in favor of the borrower.

However, recognize two logical considerations. First, credit scoring of business loans will eventually percolate through the entire banking system. The system will eventually apply to most small business loans.

From a different perspective, review the criteria that orient the credit scoring decision process. The same criteria could orient the extension of trade credit to your customer. Perhaps you do not want a formal credit scoring process, but the criteria that lend to your credit decisions would be the same. Ultimately, the reduction in losses from bad debts may justify the system.

Chapter 13

Give Your Banker Some Credit

Bank loans remain essential for the success of most independent business enterprises, but no banker approves every loan request. Bankers sometimes say "no."

The denial of any business loan request will leave you disappointed. But, a wise borrower learns from the experience. You should give your banker some credit. A loan that does not make sense for a bank may not make sense for you. The rejection of a credit request should be a signal to reevaluate the need for the bank loan.

Bankers Want to Make Loans

The interest income from business loans remains the major source of income for most banks. Declined loans add nothing to that income. So, profit oriented commercial lenders do not reject business loan requests arbitrarily.

> **Bank Note No. 33:**
> Good bank loans benefit
> the bank and the borrower.

Experienced commercial lending officers have the opportunity to review many requests for business loans. They develop the expertise necessary to identify desirable bank loans. So, some sound rationale usually justifies the rejection of a loan request. You can benefit from the effort to understand that rationale. Some examples will help illustrate that point.

Was the Loan Structured Properly?

Often, improperly structuring a loan request invites declination. A banker may decline a request for a ninety day loan to purchase equipment. You may realize benefits from that purchase, but the cash that flows from those benefits will flow in over many months. The proposed repayment is not consistent with the requested term of the loan.

From another perspective, you should not request a long-term repayment schedule for a loan that meets a short-term need. Bankers typically will not allow a twenty-four month repayment schedule for a loan designed to meet a temporary gap in your firm's cash flow. Such gaps remain temporary, so bankers want to make such loans short-term.

Experienced bankers will not reject an improperly structured loan without recourse. Instead, they will suggest structuring a loan in a manner consistent with the expected source of repayment. Those suggestions can transform a rejected loan into one that better meets your needs. You should weigh these suggestions seriously.

Similarly, bankers often defer loan requests from credit worthy firms when a borrower's own analysis of the proposal appears inadequate.

For example, before approving a loan, a banker may ask you to prepare a cash flow budget. That request serves two purposes. First, the budget will show the banker how your business can produce the cash necessary to repay the bank's loan. This will also give you some management insight on your own cash flow budget.

The process necessary to develop the budget will force you to plan for the immediate future. You must anticipate sales activity. You must predict and anticipate the need for any additional cash beyond that resulting from normal operations.

Such planning is standard for some managers, but some independent business managers lose sight of the need for planning in the midst of their daily business activities. A banker's requirement for a budget to justify a loan can help you become a better business manager.

In another instance, a banker may request a detailed schedule of your accounts receivable and inventory that will provide collateral for a proposed loan. From a banker's perspective, that detail helps insure that the receivables are collectible and that the inventory remains salable. The request should also encourage you to focus on the same considerations.

Again, the need for that management effort will appear obvious to many, but some managers focus on generating new sales more than collecting past due accounts receivable. Others allow obsolete stock to bloat their inventory.

Does the Loan Request Serve a Sensible Purpose?

On occasion, a banker may need more information about the purpose that stimulates your firm's loan request. Some requests prompt significant questions that you may overlook. The banker's queries encourage a more thorough analysis of the request. The answers help ensure that the approved loan makes sense for both the bank and the borrower.

Often, a firm declination represents the best advice a banker can provide for you. Two categories of loans stand as examples.

One category includes loan requests for speculative business purposes. Bankers typically decline such requests. Investors speculate; they hope to profit from the higher profits that can result from high risk business opportunities. From a commercial lender's perspective, the funds for that speculation should come from the investor's capital, not from bank loans. A brief illustration helps emphasize that distinction.

Assume a business has the opportunity to buy a new machine that advertises the potential for a ten-fold increase in the buyer's profits. Buying the machine calls for a $100,000 cash outlay.

Analysis shows that the potential increase in profits exists. But, the machine only has a 20 percent chance of operating as advertised. Any buyer can expect an 80 percent chance of failure.

The opportunity stands as a speculative venture. Success will provide a high return, but the purchase involves a large risk of failure.

Despite the risk, analysis may show that the business can justify buying the machine from cash on hand. Success will provide a spectacular return, but if the venture fails, the business will continue its normal operations without interruption. Since the funds for the venture come from excess cash, the loss does not become a financial obstacle to the firm's operations.

From a different perspective, assume the business lacks the funds necessary for the speculative venture. But, the firm persuades a naïve lender that the venture represents a sound, low-risk business opportunity. The lender makes the $100,000 loan necessary to proceed with the venture.

If the venture fails, the obligation to repay the bank's loan remains. That repayment must come from funds produced by its normal operations. Repayment can produce a financial strain that can threaten a firm's survival. In any circumstance, that strain limits expansion until the firm repays the loan. Using a loan to finance a speculative venture that fails can result in a major financial burden.

Of course, bankers and borrowers often have different perspectives of the speculative nature of many business loan requests. A sound premise for a loan from your perspective may appear speculative to your banker. So, a banker may decline a loan to finance a large dollar sale to an anonymous customer without verifying the buyer's credit worthiness. In another circumstance, a lender may reject a loan request for equipment necessary to manufacture an unproven product. In still another circumstance, a banker may refuse a loan to fuel an increase in sales that appears questionable.

All these declinations may result even if your financial circumstances otherwise justify the credit consideration. A good banker does not make a bad loan to the most credit worthy borrower.

Bankers can benefit borrowers by rejecting loan requests that will make a firm's debt burden excessive. That holds true even if the loan may promise to serve a prudent purpose. In any event, declining a loan request for an apparent speculative purpose may represent the proper view of your firm's best interests. A loan that is too speculative for a lender also may be too speculative for you.

Bankers typically use a firm's debt-to-equity ratio to gauge the limit on the total debt a business can have without excessive risk. That ratio rates a firm's total debt to the owner's or shareholders' equity in the business.

The debt-to-equity ratio for a business with $200,000 in debt and $100,000 in equity stands at two to one. The firm has $2 in debt for each $1 in equity used to finance its operations.

Lacking other criteria, that two-to-one ratio marks the practical limit on the debt loan a business should carry. Experience suggests that a business with a larger debt burden becomes vulnerable to unforeseen financial setbacks.

Recognizing that fact, bankers may decline loan requests when the debt would raise the borrower's debt-to-equity ratio above the two-to-one ratio noted above. Of course, a higher ratio remains acceptable in many businesses. So, do not presume that bankers decline all loans that will raise the borrower's ratio above two to one.

Also, recognize that your banker can provide a service by refusing loans that will raise your firm's debt burden too high. Independent business managers often ignore the risk that comes with debt. Their inherent optimism obscures potential problems associated with excessive debt. The banker's declination can help ensure the firm's longer term survival.

> **Bank Note No. 34:**
> Give your banker some credit.

Your banker should not decline a business loan without good reasons. On occasion, your justification for a loan may take precedence over the banker's reasons for a declination. That can justify directing the loan request elsewhere.

But most often, a banker's declination of a loan makes good business sense. So, give your banker some credit when a loan request is rejected. Declining your request may serve your firm's best interests.

Part IV

What Will You Have to Sign to Get a Loan?

Common Loan Documents

You must sign a promissory note to obtain a bank loan. The note becomes a legal obligation to repay the loan and the associated interest charges.

Additional documents become necessary when you pledge collateral to secure a loan. The common requirement for personal guaranties from the principals in a business adds another document. When a business operates as a corporation, the need for formal borrowing resolutions raises the need for still another legal document to complete the transaction.

Whatever the specific requirements, business managers do not always review the loan documents carefully before signing them. This is a common occurrence that often leads to unnecessary misunderstandings.

> **Bank Note No. 35:**
> Many managers do not review
> bank loan documents before signing them.
> They focus on their need for a bank loan.

When the documents are not examined, business managers often overlook the legal obligations that accompany a bank's credit consideration. They also fail to recognize all of a bank's legal rights if they fail to fulfill those obligations.

This chapter serves as a partial remedy to that problem. It reviews the more prominent obligations a borrower incurs from the basic agreements that govern the credit consideration a business receives from a bank.

> **Bank Note No. 36:**
> Do not view the discussion here as
> a substitute for professional legal advice.

This discussion should not be used as a substitute for legal advice, but it does address some important considerations you should recognize before signing the documents necessary to obtain a bank loan.

The Promissory Note

You must sign a note agreement to obtain a bank loan. As the central consideration in that agreement, you promise to repay the loan. So, in generic terms, the basic agreements stand as promissory notes. However, before signing a note, you should recognize the legal import of that promise to repay the loan.

> **Bank Note No. 37:**
> A promissory note becomes
> an unconditional contractual
> obligation to repay the loan.

Of course, a bank typically expects repayment by the schedule in the note. However, a promissory note gives a bank the right to demand immediate repayment of a loan as circumstances warrant.

The Interest Charge

As a logical legal requirement, a promissory note also specifies the annual percentage rate a bank charges for a loan. If a loan has a floating, or fluctuating, interest rate, the note also identifies the bench mark that spurs any upward or downward changes in the rate.

The prime lending rate set by major money center banks serves as the most common bench mark. By definition, the prime rate stands as the rate banks charge their most credit worthy customers.

But, note that the interest rate that stands as the prime rate is not the same for all banks. Each bank can set its own prime rate. The failure to recognize the bench mark can be costly.

> **Bank Note No. 38:**
> Not all bank prime lending rates are equal.

Money center banks typically have the same, publicized prime lending rates. That is the "prime rate" you probably see in the *Wall Street Journal*. But, banks not located in money centers may set higher prime rates.

For example, the prime rate for large money center banks may stand at 6 percent, but the Sample National Bank in Distant City, Arizona, may set its prime lending rate at 8 percent. A prime rate loan at the latter bank costs significantly more than one at a money center bank.

Do not assume that different prime rates among banks involves any subterfuge. Different banks can logically set different prime rates that stand as the rates they charge their most credit worthy borrowers. But, a "prime rate borrower" should recognize that different prime rates exist among banks.

The Repayment Schedule

A promissory note schedules the repayment date for the loan and its associated interest charges. The interest charge for a short-term, single payment loan usually comes due on the same date as the principal repayment schedule.

However, when a single payment loan's maturity date extends beyond ninety days, banks often require interim interest payments. Some banks expect monthly interest payments. Others look for quarterly interest payments. In either circumstance, requiring monthly or quarterly interest payments serves two purposes.

First, the payments provide banks with additional funds that can be reinvested profitably. Second, requiring periodic interest payments reminds a borrower of the debt obligation to the bank. The reminder encourages the borrower to set aside funds for the scheduled principal repayment. Requiring interim interest payments can help a borrower remain credit worthy.

A borrower pays the interest charge for an installment loan in one of two ways. The traditional installment loan includes a pre-computed interest charge in each monthly payment. Alternatively, simple interest installment loans accrue interest charges each month based on the principal balance remaining after the previous month's payment.

Banks accrue daily interest charges on the principal balances outstanding on revolving loans or lines of credit. However, banks typically expect borrowers to pay the interest charges that accumulate each month.

Late Charges

A promissory note imposes additional charges if you fail to repay your debt as scheduled. However, installment loans typically have explicit late charges for a borrower's failure to make a scheduled payment.

In contrast, promissory notes seldom include explicitly defined late charges for single payment loans that fall past due. However, if you ignore a loan's scheduled due date, you still incur late charges.

A direct charge comes from the additional interest that accrues each day until the borrower pays the note. A single payment loan's maturity date does not stop the bank's interest charges. The charges continue to accrue each day the loan remains outstanding. We can view the additional interest costs as a late charge.

Allowing a single payment loan (or any other loan) to fall past due can also impose indirect late charges. Those charges come from the damage past due loans inflict on your reputation for credit worthiness. Although you eventually make the required payment, bankers tend to question the reliability of business managers who habitually ignore or overlook scheduled loan due dates. Such questions can make future credit consideration less likely.

Default

Legally, default occurs when any party fails to observe all the tenets in a contractual agreement. A default can trigger a bank's demand for immediate repayment of a loan. That makes any potential default a serious matter.

> **Bank Note No. 39:**
> Violating any provision in a
> promissory note represents default.

You default when you fail to make any scheduled payment in a promissory note. Banks seldom take immediate action when you fail to make a payment on time, but you should recognize that any late payment still stands as a default.

Default also occurs when a creditor, other than the bank, tries to take possession of any asset a borrower has pledged as collateral for a loan. That allows a bank to step in with legal action to protect its interests.

A bankruptcy or financial failure also stands as a default by a borrower. A failing business usually lacks the ability to make its scheduled loan payments, but any default gives a bank a legal edge that may improve its chances for eventual repayment of the loan.

Of course, no promissory note can specify every event that makes up default by a borrower. From another perspective, waiting for a specified event to trigger a borrower's default may reduce a bank's chances for repayment. So, promissory notes include a discretionary clause that eliminates that potential dilemma.

> **Bank Note No. 40:**
> Promissory notes give banks
> the discretionary right to
> declare a borrower in default.

Banks can exercise the discretionary right to declare a borrower in default when events create uncertainty about a borrower's want or ability to repay a loan. A going concern making scheduled payments on time still can be in default on its debt obligations to the bank.

Allowing banks the discretionary right to declare a borrower in default may appear extreme. However, no banker enjoys perfect prescience. The discretionary right to place a borrower in default protects a bank against unforeseen events that can jeopardize the potential repayment of a loan. Declaring the business in default on its debt obligation usually remains unnecessary, but a prudent banker wants that option to exist.

As an extreme example, assume a business loses a major customer that previously accounted for 90 percent of its sales. Replacing the sales appears unlikely. That places the firm's financial circumstances, and the bank's loan, in jeopardy.

As another extreme example, assume a court convicts an equipment distributor of paying bribes to obtain sales to public agencies. The conviction clouds the firm's future. It also makes the firm's banker question the continuation of the bank's credit consideration. Using the discretionary right to place the loan in default may become a logical action necessary to improve the potential of collecting the bank's loan to the business.

The Security Agreement

You usually must pledge business collateral to secure a bank loan. That common requirement raises the need for a security agreement that ties the collateral pledged to the promissory note. That legal relationship allows the bank to take possession of the collateral pledged if you default.

> **Bank Note No. 41:**
> A security agreement ties a firm's collateral to the promissory note that marks the debt.

General Warranties

A security agreement describes the assets a business pledges to secure a bank loan. Two circumstances must exist to make the security interest that proceeds from that pledge valid. The business must own the assets pledged, and no prior liens can stand that would displace the bank's security interest.

Sometimes, banks can independently verify that those circumstances exist. For example, a registered lien appears on the owner's title when a bank makes a loan secured by an automobile or a truck. So, bankers can use the title certificate to verify ownership and show whether any prior liens exist.

Identifying prior liens becomes more difficult when a business secures a loan with accounts receivable, inventory, or equipment. Banks can search public records designed to register and reveal liens placed against those business assets, but the public records system contains some unavoidable flaws. The most diligent search may leave some liens uncovered.

A security agreement includes a provision to help protect banks against that potential oversight. By signing the security agreement, the borrower warrants that the collateral comes free of any hidden liens.

> **Bank Note No. 42:**
> Signing a security agreement when undisclosed liens exist becomes a serious legal misrepresentation.

Not disclosing all liens on assets named as collateral in a security agreement is a legal misrepresentation that can have serious consequences. Fortunately, few such misrepresentations occur.

Another general borrower warranty becomes relevant when an independent business operates as a corporation. In that event, the execution of the security agreement warrants that the corporation remains legally qualified to operate in the states where it conducts business.

Lastly, the security agreement includes a warranty that the corporation has properly authorized its execution. Executing a security agreement without the proper corporate authority again represents a legal misrepresentation of the facts.

Collateral: Evidence and Valuation

Often a bank's request for collateral to secure a loan represents an excess of caution. Little doubt exists that the business will repay the loan as scheduled. The collateral pledge shrinks that doubt further. The pledge stands as a formality.

Banks sometimes view a collateral pledge as a necessary step to insure repayment of a loan. As discussed previously, standing alone, collateral does not justify a bank loan, but collateral often becomes necessary to justify making a loan that already appears warranted. To cover those circumstances, a security agreement imposes additional obligations on a borrower that fall into two categories.

> **Bank Note No. 43:**
> A business must provide evidence
> of the value of the collateral pledged
> to secure a loan.

The business must provide evidence of the valued of the pledged collateral. Most often, a business provides that evidence in response to the bank's request. However, a security agreement gives a bank the legal right to verify collateral values on the borrower's premises. That includes the right of access, on demand, to the firm's accounting documents and records.

A security agreement also imposes obligations on a borrower to maintain the value of the collateral pledged. A sensible borrower naturally shares that objective. But, making that goal a legal requirement in a security agreement presumably adds incentive.

Conceptually, the specific collateral pledged does not alter a borrower's obligations to a bank. The business must verify and maintain the value of the collateral in any instance.

Different types of collateral change the specific steps necessary to fulfill a borrower's obligations to a bank. So, let's look at the obligations that apply to the three common categories of collateral that businesses pledge to secure bank loans-accounts receivable, inventory, and equipment.

Loans Secured by Accounts Receivable

If a security agreement pledges accounts receivable as collateral, the borrower becomes obligated to provide a complete listing of the firm's accounts receivable at the bank's request.

> **Bank Note No. 44:**
> An account receivable represents the proceeds of a completed sale on credit.

Consignment and other incomplete sales transaction do not represent true accounts receivable. Those transactions should be excluded from any account listing a business provides to a bank.

As another provision in a security agreement, a borrower warrants that the accounts included in any receivable listing represent bona fide, collectible claims against the firm's debtors. That means that the borrower must also exclude accounts subject to counter claims or offsets by a firm's customers.

The requirement for excluding questionable receivables from a firm's account listing may appear unimportant. However, the requirement does become important for a business with a loan limit set as some percentage of its bona fide accounts receivable.

To illustrate, assume a business has $100,000 in accounts receivable registered on its internal records. The firm's bank advances loans up to 80 percent of its eligible accounts receivable. At first glance, the $100,000 total qualifies the business for an $80,000 bank loan.

However, a closer look at the firm's receivables lowers the limit on the size of the loan available to the business. The firm's listing of its accounts reveals that $30,000 in receivables really represent consignment sales. The buyers have no obligation to pay the amounts due until they sell the merchandise consigned.

The firm's receivables also include $10,000 in receivables subject to counter claims from customers who also serve as suppliers to the business. Those receivables would become uncollectible if the borrower failed. Those receivables are therefore also ineligible as collateral for bank loans.

Removing the $40,000 in ineligible receivables lowers the firm's eligible accounts from $100,000 to $60,000. In turn, that drops the size of the bank loan available to the borrower from $80,000 to $48,000. The $32,000 reduction can be significant for a borrower with a tight cash flow.

The $32,000 reduction in funds available to the business also emphasizes the need to understand all the provisions in a security agreement. Ethical business managers will not expect a larger loan than a firm's eligible collateral warrants, but the limits should not come as a surprise.

Loans Secured by Inventory

An inventory security agreement gives a bank the discretionary right to request periodic reports on the collateral pledged. When a firm pledges inventory as collateral, typically banks require nothing more than a monthly or quarterly report of the accounting value of a borrower's inventory. That value already appears on the financial statements borrowers provide to a bank. So, a bank's basic reporting requirements does not represent any additional effort.

However, larger loans or loans that exceed the bounds set by traditional lending guidelines can raise the need for more stringent inventory reporting requirements. That can include reports that detail daily, weekly, or monthly movement of inventory through a business. The reports on the purchases and sales of a borrower's inventory help insure that the total collateral value remains to secure the bank's position.

> **Bank Note No. 45:**
>
> An inventory security agreement
> also requires that the borrower adequately
> insures the collateral pledged to the bank.

Assets pledged as collateral must have adequate insurance. The insurance must protect against loss or damage by fire, theft, or any other normal risks that can threaten a firm's inventory. A bank can also require additional insurance for uncommon risks that can confront some business inventory.

Ignoring the need for adequate inventory insurance may appear illogical to many business managers. Obtaining inventory insurance to protect against unforeseen catastrophe represents a prudent management practice.

Yet, some business managers try to reduce a firm's expenses by carrying a low amount of inventory insurance. Some carry no coverage. Such occurrences raise the need for the requirement for adequate insurance coverage included in inventory security agreements.

Loans Secured by Equipment

A security agreement for an equipment loan contains the same basic provisions as those for the other two types of collateral discussed above. But, equipment must meet one other requirement. Beyond basic maintenance, the security agreement obligates the borrower to repair or replace worn out or damaged parts. Of course, a prudent manager properly maintains the equipment used in his operations. But, a security agreement makes that maintenance a legal obligation.

> **Bank Note No. 46:**
>
> A borrower becomes obligated
> to keep the equipment pledged
> as collateral in good repair.

Financing Statements

A security agreement gives a bank a security interest in collateral a business pledges to secure a loan. However, a bank must also perfect its security interest in collateral for a loan.

The specific steps necessary to perfect a bank's security interest vary with the type of collateral pledged. For loans secured by business receivables, inventory, or equipment, the borrower must execute a financing statement.

The financing statement names the borrower, the bank, and the collateral pledged. The bank then files the financing statement with the appropriate state or county authority. This additional step makes the bank's lien a matter of public record. It also perfects the bank's security interest in the collateral.

Corporate Resolutions

Many independent businesses operate as corporations. A corporation stands as a legal entity apart from the principals who own the corporation's stock. So, before a corporation can borrow, the firm's board of directors must pass borrowing resolutions that authorize the business to borrow.

A bank must have a properly executed set of borrowing resolutions before making a loan to a corporation. As a practical matter, most firm's use the bank's own resolution forms as the basis for the borrowing authorization. In any event, a borrower must provide proper borrowing resolutions in a form acceptable to the bank.

Landlord's Waiver

Business inventory and equipment often serve as collateral for bank loans, thereby raising the need for security agreements and financing statements besides the bank's promissory notes. However, a landlord's waiver also becomes necessary for businesses operating on leased premises.

> **Bank Note No. 48:**
> Banks require a landlord's waiver when making a loan secured by business equipment or inventory used in leased premises.

A waiver insures that the bank has access to the collateral pledged if the borrower defaults. By signing the waiver, a lessor, or landlord, agrees to allow a bank to enter the leased premises to repossess the inventory or equipment pledged as collateral.

A bank's requirement for a landlord's waiver can become a point of contention. After all, a business contending with financial difficulties may fall behind in its lease payments. So, a lessor may want the right to claim a lessee's assets in case of default on the lease. That can make a lessor reluctant to sign a landlord's waiver.

This potential problem seldom changes a bank's requirement for the waiver. The waiver will remain a necessary precedent for a loan secured by business inventory and equipment.

The Personal Guaranty

As a standard requirement, banks expect personal guaranties for loans to independent businesses. As a minimum requirement, a bank will expect the principal shareholder in a business to guarantee any loans to the firm. At the other extreme, a bank will expect guaranties from all the firm's shareholders. In community property states, that may also include personal guaranties from the husbands or wives of the principal shareholders in the business.

Chapter 15

Special Loan Agreements

Banks commonly commit to revolving loans and lines of credit for periods that extend up to one year. On occasion, banks make commitments that extend longer. When banks make such commitments, they often seek more protection than comes from the basic loan documents discussed in the previous chapter.

> **Bank Note No. 49:**
> Longer term bank credit commitments may raise the need for special loan agreements.

Special loan agreements establish financial and operating guidelines a business must observe to retain a bank's commitment to provide the revolving loan or line of credit. Violating guidelines in a loan agreement can lead to the demand for immediate repayment of the bank's loan.

Banks tailor loan agreements to fit each borrower's circumstances, but some financial and operating guidelines remain common to almost every special loan agreement. This chapter reviews those guidelines. The discussion also touches on the premises that, from a banker's perspective, justify the need to place financial and operating constraints on a business borrower.

The Credit Commitment

A loan agreement does not alter any of the obligations in a bank's promissory notes. Nor do any of the requirements set forth in a bank's security agreements change. Instead, a loan agreement details additional requirements or restrictions designed to fit each borrower's unique circumstances.

As a common example, loan agreements often detail the definition of the collateral value a business pledges to secure a bank's loan and may limit the amount of a loan to a specific percentage or portion of the value of the pledged collateral.

> **Bank Note No. 50:**
> A loan agreement may limit advances for secured loans to a portion of the value of the collateral pledged.

For example, a loan agreement might specify that the outstanding principal balance on a revolving loan shall not exceed the lesser of:
1. The sum of $1,000,000, or
2. The sum equal to:
    a. 80 percent of the borrower's receivables less than sixty days old, plus
    b. 50 percent of the book value of the borrower's inventory.

The $1,000,000 in this instance represents the maximum loan available under the terms of the loan agreement. However, relating the potential loan to the collateral pledged could limit the borrower to a loan below that maximum.

To illustrate, assume that the borrower in this instance begins a month with $600,000 in eligible accounts receivable, i.e., those less than sixty days old. The firm also has $500,000 in inventory on hand as the month begins. Based on the above limits, we can find the maximum credit consideration available to the business as:

Advance against receivables:	$600,000 x 80%	=	$480,000
Advance against inventory:	$500,000 x 50%	=	$250,000
Maximum credit consideration:		=	$730,000

The potential $1,000,000 in total credit consideration in this instance remains intact. But, the loan agreement makes that potential subject to the limits set by the collateral advance rates. Based on the above collateral values, that drops the maximum bank credit consideration available to the borrower down to $730,000.

Restricting advances to a portion of a firm's collateral value relates a bank's credit exposure to a borrower's real needs. A higher volume that increases a firm's inventory and receivables also makes more bank funds available. A lower volume should reduce the need for those funds. Relating a bank's loan to a firm's collateral makes those reductions a requirement.

Reporting Requirements

Banks expect borrowers to provide copies of their current balance sheets and income statements. Many also expect to see copies of a borrower's tax returns. Those requirements help support the validity of the firm's accounting statements. In any event, loan agreements make those requirements explicit.

> **Bank Note No. 51:**
> Loan agreements may specify
> a firm's financial reporting requirements.

An agreement may require a business to provide a bank with copies of its financial statements each month or each quarter. Moreover, to encourage compliance, an agreement may require receipt of the statements within a stated length of time.

For example, a common requirement calls for financial statements within thirty days after the end of each quarter of a firm's operations. Failure to provide the statements represents another event that becomes default by a borrower.

Another common requirement included in some loan agreements calls for annual financial statements audited by certified public accountants. That requirement helps insure that a bank receives valid financial information from a major business borrower.

This requirement does not imply any distrust of a borrower. Instead, it helps reinforce the reliability of the firm's own internal accounting system. Of course, when inadequacies exist, the audited statements help provide the correct financial information necessary for both the bank and the business.

A loan agreement may also include explicit requirements for personal financial statements from the guarantors for the business loan. That enables the bank to monitor the financial viability of the guarantors.

When collateral pledges exist, loan agreements often have additional reporting requirements. A business using receivables as collateral usually has to provide a monthly aging analysis of those accounts. That enables the bank to find the appropriate limit on the funds the business can obtain within the collateral limits.

Similarly, a loan partially secured by inventory raises the need for inventory reporting requirements. A borrower may have to provide periodically an accounting measure of its inventory. Or, in more extreme circumstances, a borrower may have to provide a specific listing of the inventory to the bank. In the most extreme circumstances, a special loan agreement will include a requirement for periodic physical counts of a borrower's inventory.

Some agreements will require an independent accountant's participation in the counts. In other instances, the requirement may be for a banker's participation. Such counts help ensure the collateral value of the inventory pledged to secure the bank's loan.

Operating Restrictions

A bank extending a longer term credit commitment wants to ensure that management continues to operate prudently. The bank encourages that prudence in special loan agreements, which often specify operating restrictions. These restrictions seldom interfere with a firm's normal operations. Instead, they focus on management actions that can materially alter a firm's financial circumstances.

> **Bank Note No. 52:**
> Special loan agreements often place
> operating restrictions on a business.

As a common example, loan agreements usually bar a business from incurring any additional debt obligations. That restriction does not usually apply to trade credit the business receives from suppliers. Rather, it precludes additional loans from other financial institutions. This bar against additional financing helps a bank exercise some influence over a borrower's financial circumstances.

Bankers do not want to become involved in their borrowers' daily operations, but a bank providing the bulk of a firm's financing wants protection against imprudent management actions. A restriction against loans from other lenders helps provide some of that protection.

Note that the above restriction does not eliminate the possibility for new financing. But, the restriction gives the bank the right to review the firm's justification for any new loan. The bank also retains the right to veto the loan request.

Another common restriction found in loan agreements precludes a borrower from standing as a guarantor for loans to any other individual or entity. Such guaranties increase a firm's contingent liabilities and its financial vulnerability. That, in turn, raises the risk associated with the bank's loan. Prohibiting such guaranties help preserve a borrower's credit worthiness.

> **Bank Note No. 53:**
> Bankers want their borrowers
> to concentrate on their primary
> business activities.

To encourage borrowers to concentrate on their primary business activities, loan agreements may prevent a firm from engaging in any new or different activities that depart significantly from its main business. So, as a logical complement, special loan agreements often include a provision that prevents a borrower from buying or merging with another business. That helps prevent significant changes that might impair a firm's ability to repay its bank credit consideration.

Banks also want continuity in the management of a business enterprise with an extended credit commitment. After all, a banker's view of a borrower's credit worthiness rests largely on the display of management ability in a business. Any changes in upper management can affect that ability. So, loan agreements allow banks to make a judgment on management changes without any obligation to continue existing credit consideration.

> **Bank Note No. 54:**
> Special loan agreements typically include significant changes in a firm's management.

As a practical matter, the above operating restrictions seldom become onerous for businesses. Most business managers already want to focus on the firm's main activities. Few become concerned with mergers or acquisitions of other businesses. Without severe setbacks, managers persevere in their jobs. Moreover, banks can waive any restriction in a special loan agreement when circumstances warrant. Waivers are common when a special opportunity makes good business sense for a borrower.

Financial Restrictions

Only financially strong borrowers receive extended commitments for bank lines of credit. However, banks want to encourage those borrowers to maintain that financial strength, so bankers often place financial restrictions on the borrower in the loan agreement. The specific restrictions naturally vary with the circumstances, but the more common restrictions develop logically from the credit criteria bankers use to evaluate a borrower's financial standing.

> **Bank Note No. 55:**
> A loan agreement may place financial restrictions on a borrower.

For example, loan agreements usually set ratio requirements that encourage borrowers to maintain enough liquidity to meet their current obligations. Meeting that liquidity requirement can also help borrowers overcome most unforeseen financial setbacks. Bankers typically use the current and quick ratios to set the liquidity requirements included in loan agreements.

A loan agreement may specify that a borrower must maintain no less than a 2.0 current ratio and a 1.0 quick ratio. Allowing either ratio to fall below those minimum levels violates the loan agreement. The bank then has the right to make any loans to the business immediately due and payable.

As a practical matter, banks rarely exercise that right. They commonly waive a borrower's violation of the financial restrictions included in loan agreements. But, banks do not extend waivers haphazardly. Instead, waivers represent a logical response to a borrower's affirmative effort to remedy the violation. Should the remedy not develop, the bank retains its right to accelerate payment of the debt.

Another financial restriction common in special loan agreements imposes limits on the total debt obligation a borrower can incur. That restriction appears most often as a limit on a firm's maximum debt-to-equity ratio.

For example, a loan agreement may specify that the borrower will not allow the ratio of its total debt to its net worth rise above a two-to-one relationship. That limits the firm to $2 in debt for each $1 in shareholders' equity.

Bankers seek such limits because aggressive managers often ignore the financial risks that accompany any increase in debt. Placing limits on a firm's debt-to-equity ratio helps limit the debt burden and the risk a borrower can take.

Loan agreements may also include provisions designed to preserve the stockholders' equity in the business. For example, one common provision restricts or precludes dividend payments to shareholders. Another common provision prohibits the business from buying shareholders' interests. Such provisions help maintain a firm's equity and help prevent shareholders from draining funds from the business.

Some loan agreements also require borrowers to operate profitably. At first glance, that may seem an odd requirement. After all, every business manager wants to operate profitably. But, the requirement sets another standard to encourage prudent management. A business can satisfy all the other financial guidelines in a loan agreement but still fail to operate profitably. The requirement for profitable operations then becomes another logical provision in loan agreements.

The review here does not exhaust the financial restrictions a bank's special loan agreements can place on a borrower. A borrower's particular circumstances make other, more complete restrictions necessary. However, this review does cover the more common examples.

Potential Waivers

The potential restrictions in loan agreements discussed above may appear excessive to many business managers. You may view some of those restrictions as excessive intrusions that limit the firm's options. That view becomes valid if bankers expect perfect observance of all the restrictions set forth in loan agreements.

But, banks and bankers acknowledge their inability to foresee the future. They recognize that a change in a firm's circumstances can make the restrictions included in some loan agreements illogical. That leads to a provision in loan agreements and the banks ability to waive any violation of the restrictions set forth. Any waiver remains an option, but waivers are common when the requests do not appear to affect the prospects for eventual repayment of the bank's credit consideration.

> **Bank Note No. 56:**
> Loan agreements allow the bank to waive a firm's violation of any restriction included in an agreement.

As an important consideration, the need for a waiver of a requirement or restriction should not arise after the fact. Bankers are often agreeable to waivers that result from sensible requests before a violation of a provision in a loan agreement. Bankers become less agreeable when a borrower asks for a waiver after the firm's actions have already violated the agreement.

Default

A loan agreement does not alter the events that represent a borrower's default as specified in a bank's standard loan and security agreements.

Each additional requirement in a special agreement becomes an addition to the standard list. Violating any requirement becomes another event that stands as a default.

The failure to provide financial statements as specified in a special loan agreement places a borrower in default, so does violation of any other requirement. Special loan agreements never enhance a borrower's position. On the contrary, they always place a bank in better position to gain repayment of the credit consideration extended to a business.

Before You Sign

You should recognize two important facts before signing any special loan agreement. First, the provisions in such agreements become legally binding. You should fully understand the prominent provisions affecting your firm's circumstances. So, you should closely review a special loan agreement before you sign. Seek help from a qualified attorney. The need for that foresight appears logical. Yet, many business managers focus only on a bank's potential credit consideration. They ignore the restrictions that accompany that consideration.

That oversight encumbers many borrowers with operating and financial restrictions that become onerous. Without contention, bankers will always include more restrictive conditions in special loan agreements.

That leads to the second fact about loan agreements business managers should recognize. Until executed, the major provisions in loan agreements remain subject to negotiation. Bankers have one perception of the restrictions necessary in a special loan agreement; borrowers often have another. Resolution of any disagreements does not automatically fall in the banker's favor.

You should feel comfortable with the specific requirements included in a special loan agreement. You should not accept a bank's requirement for a two-to-one current ratio when a one-to-one ratio is more appropriate for your business. Nor should you accept a restrictive debt-to-equity ratio that unnecessarily restricts your options without really enhancing the bank's position.

Of course, the outcome of any negotiations will vary. Financially strapped borrowers will more readily agree to a bank's restrictions.

Borrowers under less financial pressure enjoy a stronger negotiating stance. But, realize that the potential for negotiation does exist, and negotiation should precede your execution of any special loan agreement.

Part V

What Will It Cost You to Borrow from a Bank?

The Direct Cost
of a Bank Loan

Before obtaining a bank loan, a thoughtful manager weighs the cost of borrowing against the expected benefits. The three closing chapters in this book will help you with that task.

This chapter discusses the direct interest charges a business pays for bank loans. However, those charges seldom represent the total cost a business pays for bank credit consideration.

> **Bank Note No. 57:**
> The total cost of a bank loan
> exceeds the direct interest charges.

The following chapter reviews the other considerations that can make the total cost of a bank loan larger than it first appears. That total should naturally stand as the relevant cost in a firm's borrowing decision.

The final chapter then provides some different views of the potential benefits a business can receive from bank loans. The most important view suggests that you should ignore interest rates as a consideration in the business borrowing decision. You will find that making interest rates the focal point of the borrowing decision can become an expensive mistake.

The Direct Cost of a Single Payment Loan

To set the foundation for discussion, we will look at the logical approach to calculating the charge for a single payment loan. This approach uses the simple interest rate calculation.

To illustrate, assume a bank charges a 12 percent annual percentage rate for a $100,000 single payment loan extended to a business for a full year. The interest charge calculation in that instance becomes:

$$\text{Loan} \quad \text{x} \quad \text{Annual Interest Rate} \quad = \quad \text{Interest Charge}$$
$$\$100,000 \quad \text{x} \quad 12\% \quad = \quad \$12,000$$

The borrower incurs a $12,000 interest charge for using the $100,000 bank loan for a full year.

Logical as it appears, this view only approximates the actual process banks use to calculate the interest charge for a single payment loan.

The Daily Rental Rate

Banks typically do not make single payment loans that extend for a full year. Ninety days stands as the most common term. Of course, shorter and longer terms also exist.

In any event, banks do not directly use an annual percentage rate to calculate the interest charge for a single payment loan. Instead, they use a daily interest rate.

> **Bank Note No. 58:**
> Banks charge a daily interest rate
> for the funds borrowed in
> a single payment loan.

Banks convert the annual percentage charge for a single payment loan into a daily interest charge. The daily charge applies to each dollar for each day a business uses the borrowed funds.

To illustrate, assume a bank charges a 12 percent annual percentage rate for a ninety-day single payment loan to a business.

To find the interest charge for the loan, the bank first converts the annual percentage rate to a daily percentage rate:

$$\frac{\text{Annual percentage rate}}{365} = \text{Daily percentage rate}$$

$$\frac{10\%}{365} = .0002739\% \text{ per day}$$

The 10% annual percentage rate translates into a .0002739% daily interest charge. The bank charges that daily rate for each dollar for each day the borrower uses the bank's funds.

Using that daily interest charge, the process that finds a bank's charge for a $100,000, ninety-day single payment loan then follows:

Loan x Daily Interest x Number of Days = Interest Charge
          Rate   Outstanding

$100,000   x   .0002739%   x   90   = $2,465.10

In this instance, the daily charge for the $100,000 loan for ninety days accumulates to $2,465.10.

You gain a useful management perspective by viewing a bank's daily interest charge in a manner analogous to the daily fixed charge for renting a car. The bank's interest charge becomes the rental rate for each dollar the borrower uses each day.

Recognizing that perspective can encourage a manager to control his use of borrowed funds. Focusing on the annual percentage rate on a loan really is not useful for day to day financial management. The real dollar cost for the borrowed funds is the relevant consideration.

Prepaying a Single Payment Loan

A bank charges a daily interest rate for the dollars advanced in a single payment loan. This practice clearly benefits the business that can repay a single payment loan before it matures, by reducing interest charges. This is true even when a business prepays only part of the loan before it matures.

Bank Note No. 59:
Prepaying a single payment loan
reduces a borrower's interest charges.

To illustrate the potential benefits, assume a bank agrees to make a $100,000 single payment loan to a business for 120 days. The bank's 10 percent annual rate translates into a .0002739% daily charge. So, the borrower's total interest charge for using the $100,000 for the full 120 days is $3,286.89.

Later, the business finds that it does not need the $100,000 for the full 120-day term of the single payment loan. The firm generates enough cash to repay the bank $25,000 each month. In that event, the interest charge calculation process for the loan becomes:

Loan Balance		Days Outstanding		Daily Interest Rate		Interest Charge
$100,000	x	30	x	.0002739	=	$ 821.70
$ 75,000	x	30	x	.0002739	=	$ 616.28
$ 50,000	x	30	x	.0002739	=	$ 410.85
$ 25,000	x	30	x	.0002739	=	$ 205.42
						$2,054.25

Repaying the original $100,000 loan with $25,000 monthly payments reduces the firm's interest charges to $2,054.25. That represents a $1,232.55 reduction below the charges for keeping the full $100,000 loan for 120 days. The potential savings should encourage you to take advantage of any opportunity to prepay a significant portion of a single payment loan.

Some caution should also intervene. Using funds for repayment that a business may soon need for other requirements remains unwise. Keeping the cash and paying the additional interest charges often stands as the best financial management alternative.

Floating Rates vs. Fixed Rates

The distinction between fixed and floating interest rates stands as another factor that can affect the direct cost of a single payment or revolving loan.

A fixed interest rate remains constant for the term of a loan. The general level of interest rates may move up or down, but a fixed rate attached to a loan does not change.

In contrast, a floating interest rate can fluctuate during the term of a loan. Any fluctuation usually occurs in line with some visible bench mark. The prevailing prime lending rate usually serves as that bench mark.

For example, an interest charge set two points above prime translates into a 9 percent rate when the prime rate stands at 7 percent. If the prime moves up, so will the borrower's interest charge. When the prime rises to 20 percent, the business loan will carry a 22 percent annual rate. The borrower's interest rate will also fall as the prime drops below the 7 percent level.

Not all banks offer a borrower the option to choose between a fixed or floating interest charge. However, when the option exists, the offer typically includes a fixed rate that is higher than the floating rate on the date of the loan.

To illustrate, assume the prevailing prime interest rate stands at 7 percent. A bank may offer to extend a business loan that allows a borrower to choose between an 11 percent fixed rate and a floating rate set two points above the prime rate. If the borrower chooses the floating rate, the interest charge becomes 9 percent. Of course, a significant rise in the prime rate can raise the borrower's floating rate above the 11 percent fixed rate.

Some straightforward logic should orient the choice between a fixed or floating interest rate on a loan. If you expect the general level of interest rates to fall, you should select the floating interest rate. When the rates later fall, you will reap the benefits from a lower borrowing cost. Alternatively, if you expect interest rates to rise, you should choose the fixed rate loan. If interest later rises, you will remain locked into the lower fixed rate.

In any event, the logic that should orient the choice between a fixed and floating rate on a loan remains difficult to use in practice.

That logic rests on the premise that you can accurately predict fluctuations in the general level of interest rates. However, unpredictable fluctuations in interest rates have become the norm in the modern economy. That unpredictability undermines the logic that should orient the choice between a fixed and floating interest rate.

Some business managers rely heavily on economic analyses that predict interest rate movements. Those managers can use the preceding discussion as the basis for choosing between a fixed and floating interest rate on a loan.

A business manager's disposition toward risk can also become a consideration in the choice between a fixed and floating rate loan. A risk averse manager will usually feel more comfortable with a fixed rate loan. Fixed rates make a firm's interest charges predictable. They eliminate concern about any fluctuations in interest rates. The freedom from concern can justify the point or two differential above the prevailing floating rate.

Managers more comfortable with risk will find floating interest rates more acceptable. The potential cost advantage from the lower floating rate compensates for the risk that the rate can rise above the alternative fixed rate.

Negotiating Interest Rates

Some business managers make interest rates a contentious issue. They badger their bankers to reduce the interest rates on their business loans. Unfortunately, that practice can severely scar a banking relationship. Obviously, lower interest rates reduce a firm's borrowing costs, but three reasons make significant concern about the particular interest rate on any loan unnecessary.

> **Bank Note No. 60:**
> Making interest rates a point of contention
> undermines the financial partnership
> between a business and a bank.

First, thoughtful bankers do not casually overcharge their customers. The natural forces of competition encourage bankers to charge competitive interest rates. A bank cannot hold its interest rates significantly above those charged by its competitors. That practice would inevitably drive away some existing customers and make attracting new business more difficult.

Moreover, most bankers are fair, reasonable people. They have no incentive to charge their customers more than fair, reasonable interest rates. Most bankers want a mutually rewarding relationship with their customers.

Unfortunately, many borrowers expect lower rates than they deserve. They forget that a firm's deposits influence the interest rate its bank charges for loans. A business that maintains a low average deposit level must compensate by paying higher interest rates for its bank loans. Carrying a higher level of deposits earns a business the right to lower interest rates. Recognizing deposit and other business considerations, you can usually assume that your banker will charge a fair interest rate for the bank's loans to your business. Haggling over interest rates inevitably implies questions about the banker's integrity.

The second factor that should discourage managers from being overly concerned with interest rates centers on the benefits a business gains from bank loans. To justify borrowing, the expected benefits from a loan should far exceed the interest costs. In this case, close does not count. The benefits should be large enough to absorb an interest charge that is 1/2 to 1 percent above what a borrower expects.

After all, a 1 percent higher interest charge adds only $1,000 to the cost of a $100,000 single payment loan extended for a full year. The benefits from the loan should easily be significant enough to absorb the difference. If not, the loan may not be justifiable in any circumstance.

The final reason that should discourage excessive concern about interest rates returns us to the premise that opens the book. A successful banking relationship grows into a financial partnership between a business and a bank. Ideally, the partnership becomes a mutually profitable relationship that extends over a long period.

Some businesses will gain above average profits from the relationship. At other times, the bank may gain some interest income that represents an above average return. But, over the longer term, the benefits provide ample reward for both members of the partnership.

The manager who needlessly haggles over interest rates today ignores the longer term perspective of the financial partnership between a business and a bank. From a banker's perspective, such haggling can become a point of contention that erodes the strength of the partnership. When it persists, a banker may suggest the dissolution of the partnership.

The Total Cost of a Bank Loan

Not all the costs of bank loans become apparent in the interest charges. Some indirect costs make bank financing more expensive than many business managers realize. Do not misunderstand. Bankers do not intentionally mislead borrowers about the costs associated with a bank loan. They readily discuss the factors that raise the total cost of a bank loan above the apparent cost. This chapter will help prepare you for that discussion.

> **Bank Note No. 61:**
> The total cost of a bank loan exceeds the direct interest charges.

It is important to have that discussion, because some factors that raise the cost of a bank loan remain negotiable. Informed borrowers can use that fact to reduce the indirect costs associated with bank credit consideration.

The Compensating Balance Requirement

Banks often set compensating balance requirements for business borrowers. Such a requirement makes a borrower carry deposits equivalent to some portion of the bank loan to the business. Compensating balance requirements help banks garner funds that can be used for profitable investment elsewhere. Compensating balances enable a bank to make more loans than would otherwise be possible.

However, a borrower should view a compensating balance requirement from a different perspective. A compensating balance requirement forces a business to borrow more than it really needs.

> **Bank Note No. 62:**
> A compensating balance requirement
> raises a firm's cost of borrowing.

For example, a business that needs $400,000 in total funds may have to borrow $500,000 to satisfy a bank's requirement for a 20 percent compensating balance. The firm pays for $100,000 in credit consideration that sits idly in its checking account.

Meeting the requirement for a compensating balance becomes part of the contribution a business makes to the financial partnerships with its bank. But, you should recognize how that requirement affects the cost of a bank loan. To measure that effect, relate the actual dollar cost of a bank loan to the net borrowed funds your business uses out of the loan.

For example, assume a bank approves a $100,000 single payment loan to a business, repayable at the end of one year. The bank charges a 10 percent annual percentage rate for that credit consideration and also requires a 20 percent compensating balance for the term of the loan.

We find the effective cost of the loan as follows:

$$\text{Effective Cost of Loan} = \frac{\text{Actual Dollar Interest Cost}}{\text{Net Borrowed Funds}}$$

$$\text{Effective Cost of Loan} = \frac{\$10,000}{\$80,000} = 12.5\%$$

The inability to use 20 percent of the total bank credit consideration raises the firm's apparent cost of borrowing by $2\frac{1}{2}$ percent above the direct 10 percent interest charge.

Table 16-1 charts the effect of various compensating balance requirements across a range of interest rates. Logically, either higher interest rates or higher compensative balance requirements have a larger effect on a firm's borrowing costs.

Some business managers make a questionable boast. They assert that their bankers do not make a compensating balance a requirement of a loan. Their banks presumably make loans without attaching any compensating balance requirements.

Such assertions defy logic. Achieving a reasonable yield from its loans remains a necessity for any bank's profitable operation. That makes a firm's compensating balance a consideration in every interest rate decision on every significant business loan.

So, more logically, a banker's silence about compensating balances represents a signal that a borrower's deposits exceed the bank's normal requirements. A compensating balance requirement spurs discussion only when a firm's normal deposit levels prove inadequate.

Table 17-1: Effect of Compensating Balances on the Cost of Borrowing

		Compensating Balance Requirements		
		10%	20%	30%
	8%	8.8	10.0	11.4
Stated Interest Rate	9%	10.0	11.25	12.8
	10%	11.1	12.5	14.3
	11%	12.2	13.8	15.7
	12%	13.3	15.0	17.1
		True Annual Percentage Rate		

Commitment Fees

Businesses often obtain lines of credit merely to protect against potential cash demands raised by unforeseen problems. Such foresight represents good business sense. However, that foresight can result in a cost of borrowing even if the business never uses the committed funds.

A fee for establishing a line of credit typically totals 1/4% to 1/2% of the unused portion of the approved line. So, a business that uses only $100,000 out of a $200,000 line of credit will pay an interest charge for the borrowed funds. But, the business will also pay a $250 to $500 fee for the funds committed but not employed. A commitment fee may be a small price to pay for access to borrowed funds, but recognize that it becomes another cost of bank credit consideration.

Note also that banks often set compensating balance requirements that relate to the unused portion of a firm's line of credit. For example, a bank may expect a business with a $500,000 line of credit to maintain compensating balances equivalent to 10 percent of the unused portion of the line. The compensating balance requirement then rises to 20 percent of any funds the bank advances to the business on the credit line.

So, when the business is not using the line, the compensating balance requirement stands at $50,000. When the business draws the full $500,000 available on the line, the compensating balance requirement rises to $100,000. While the business uses less than the full $500,000 available from the line, the compensating balance requirement falls between those extremes.

We cannot measure the direct cost of the compensating balance required for an unused line of credit. That cost really comes indirectly from the inability to invest the necessary balances profitably. But, we can recognize that such requirements add to the total cost of bank credit consideration.

Legal Fees

Standardized forms document most bank loans to businesses. Neither the banks nor the borrowers involve attorneys in the transactions. So, no legal fees arise. However, many banks charge documentation fees to cover the administrative costs associated with preparing the loan documents. You should view them as another part of the unavoidable cost of borrowing.

More complex lending arrangements can raise the need for the special loan agreements discussed in chapter 14. A bank's legal firm usually prepares the agreements that govern these special transactions. So, legal fees naturally follow, and those fees add to the total cost of bank credit consideration because the bank will pass those fees on to the borrower.

> **Bank Note No. 64:**
> Banks pass legal fees on
> to their borrowers.

A straightforward premise presumably justifies passing legal fees onto a borrower. From a banker's perspective, no fees would arise without the special loan agreement. The borrower's circumstances make the special agreements necessary to justify the bank's credit consideration. So, the borrower should pay the resulting legal fees. Sometimes, the legal fees associated with a larger, more complicated transaction may become a negotiable consideration between a bank and a borrower.

We should also recognize that a borrower may incur legal fees besides those passed through by the bank. That occurs when a borrower uses an attorney to review a bank's special loan agreement. While that step is often a useful measure of prudence, it also adds to the total cost of a bank loan.

Filing Fees

Chapter 14 discusses the basic loan agreements that govern a bank loan to a business. That discussion includes a look at the financing statements lenders use to perfect a security interest in collateral a borrower pledges to secure a loan.

Of course, the statements must be filed with the appropriate county or state agencies to become legally effective. Banks usually pass the cost of the filing fees on to their borrowers. Usually, the filing fees remain modest, but they become another addition to the cost of borrowing from a bank.

Insurance Requirements

Inventory or equipment secures many bank loans to businesses. To protect the collateral value of that security, banks usually expect a borrower to carry an adequate level of property damage insurance.

At first glance, a bank's requirement for that insurance does not become an addition to a firm's borrowing cost, because thoughtful managers already carry property damage insurance on the firm's tangible assets. However, bankers and borrowers often disagree upon what makes up an adequate level of insurance protection, so additional insurance may need to be purchased before securing a loan.

For example, a hardware distributor with $500,000 in inventory may carry only $200,000 in insurance protection. Management can argue logically that the non-perishable nature of the inventory makes a higher level of protection unnecessary. But, a bank may require full insurance coverage before making a loan secured by the firm's inventory. That may come from a higher amount of protection that still falls below the full value of the firm's inventory, but raising the level of protection will raise the firm's premium and become another additional cost associated with the loan.

Another common insurance banks require is life insurance on the key managers of the business. The business is required to pledge the life insurance to the bank as additional collateral for a loan. The bank then becomes the beneficiary of the proceeds of the policy. Of course, the proceeds to the bank cannot exceed the size of the debt obligation due from the business. Any proceeds that exceed the bank's loan reverts to the secondary beneficiary named in the policy.

> **Bank Note No. 65:**
> Banks often require life insurance on the
> key managers in a business enterprise.

The requirement for life insurance often accompanies loans to closed corporations. A single individual, the major shareholder, usually stands as the predominate force in such firms. However successful such a business becomes, the premature death of the principal can mark the end of the enterprise. That fact makes the requirement for life insurance on the principal a logical step to add a measure of protection for the bank's interests.

As a practical matter, a closed corporation should carry life insurance on key managers, so pledging part of that protection as additional security on a bank loan does not necessarily add to the cost of borrowing. However, that requirement becomes an additional cost when the insurance is not already in place.

The Cost of Financial and Operating Restrictions

Special loan agreements often govern larger, more complicated bank loans to businesses. As discussed in chapter 15, those agreements usually place financial and operating constraints on a business. The constraints presumably help maintain a borrower's credit consideration. However, these restrictions can also increase the cost of bank consideration. This occurs when a financial or operating restriction precludes actions that can be profitable for a business.

> **Bank Note No. 66:**
> Financial and operating restrictions
> can increase the cost of
> bank credit consideration.

For example, a restriction against incurring additional debt may force a business to forego a profitable acquisition. A restriction against changing a firm's primary operations may force a borrower to pass up a profitable opportunity in a new market. A maximum debt-to-equity ratio restriction can prevent a business from benefiting from a special quantity buy offered by a major supplier.

A bank can waive any financial or operating restriction that hampers a borrower. However, while waiting for that waiver, the business might lose a profitable business opportunity to a competitor with the capacity for prompt action. No matter how much promise an opportunity may hold, the bank may ultimately refuse to waive the restrictions. The business may find its potential limited or stymied altogether.

The cost of operating and financial restrictions may be difficult to measure, but it can become a larger addition to the cost of a bank loan. Remember that fact before you accept such binding credit.

The Cost of Negotiating Renewals

Often a business is unable to retire a single payment loan as originally agreed. The purpose that justified the loan may remain unfulfilled, or a changing business environment requires a decision that absorbs the cash earmarked for the repayment.

The failure to meet the repayment obligation is seldom a cause for serious concern if the borrower maintains the appropriate credit worthiness. However, negotiating an extension or renewal of the loan becomes another element in the cost of bank financing. You measure that cost in terms of the management time devoted to the negotiating process.

If negotiating a renewal requires no more than a phone call or a brief visit to the bank, the cost is small. It can be considered as part of your normal operating expenses. But, as the management time devoted to obtaining renewals (or new loans) increases, the cost of negotiating rises rapidly.

After all, you cannot use your management talents when engaged in loan negotiations. Too much time negotiating for credit consideration can damage your firm's earnings. The more valuable your time, the larger the cost of negotiating renewals.

The Cost of Annual Cleanups

Many banks expect its borrowers to repay all loans and operate free of any bank credit consideration for thirty to ninety days each year. This requirement for an annual cleanup period can become another element in the true cost of credit consideration

This requirement does not pose a problem for the seasonal business. The natural business cycle generates the cash necessary to satisfy the cleanup requirement. However, the business with a level or expanding sales volume may find the requirement a burden. A business either must obtain comparable credit consideration elsewhere, usually from trade creditors, or temporarily scale down its operations.

If the burden falls on trade creditors, the business may lose trade discounts that it previously took with the aid of the bank financing. In the extreme circumstance, the business may suffer injury to its credit rating. This can restrict future operations even further. Alternatively, should the business scale down its operations for the cleanup period, it will suffer another opportunity cost-the potential profits on lost sales. In either case, the cleanup period can prove costly.

Measuring the Benefits from a Bank Loan

The total cost of any bank credit consideration exceeds the interest charges for a loan, but the interest charge still stands as the largest proportion of that cost. So, that charge also remains the largest concern for the business borrower.

However, many business managers view the interest cost associated with a bank loan from the wrong perspective. They focus on the interest rate a bank sets for its loans. However, a manager makes a serious mistake when the interest rate becomes the focal point in a business decision, because the interest rate really is irrelevant. At first glance, you will question that claim. After all, interest charges affect a firm's earnings. Higher interest rates result in higher interest charges.

> **Bank Note No. 67:**
> The interest rate on a loan is irrelevant.

But, the specific interest rate on a loan should not become the focal point of the borrowing decision. What matters is the total dollar cost of the borrowed funds and the total dollar benefits your business gains from using those funds. This is true whether the interest rate attached to a loan stands at 10 percent, 20 percent, or even higher.

To prove that claim, let's look at some common reasons why businesses borrow. These examples will also help illustrate how to measure the benefits a business can realize from bank loans.

Earning Supplier Profits

Many businesses use bank loans to take advantage of supplier profits. The cash from such loans enables the businesses to use payment practices that result in lower net purchase costs. When used effectively, a business moves some of its suppliers' profits into its own earnings. One potential source of those profits comes from the cash discounts some suppliers allow for the early payment of a firm's purchases.

> **Bank Note No. 68:**
> A business can use a bank loan to take cash discounts suppliers allow for early payment.

A brief look at the Bonner Corporation illustrates how a loan can be used to take advantage of potential supplier benefits.

The Bonner Corporation purchases $200,000 in merchandise each month to maintain its inventory at a level appropriate for its sales volume. A number of the firm's suppliers offer a 2 percent discount for payment within ten days, requiring payment in full in thirty days. Bonner now misses the 2 percent discounts but has adequate cash flow to pay for purchases in thirty days. Assuming that half of the monthly $200,000 in inventory comes from these ten day discount suppliers, the discounts lost reduce the firm's annual earnings as follows:

$$\$1,200,000 \quad x \quad 2\% \quad = \quad \$24,000$$

The failure to take the 2 percent discounts costs the Bonner Corporation $24,000 per year. Recognizing that fact, management decides to obtain a bank loan to gain the funds necessary to take the 2 percent discounts.

The 2 percent discounts are available on $100,000 of Bonner's monthly purchases. Of course, ten day discount purchases can remain outstanding as accounts payable any time. So, Bonner needs to borrow only $66,666, i.e., two-thirds of the monthly total, to take advantage of the available discounts.

If the firm incurs a 12 percent annual interest charge, we can calculate the net dollar benefits from the bank loan as follows:

Total Annual Discounts Taken	$24,000
Annual Borrowing Cost	8,000
($66,666) x 12%	
Net Dollar Benefit	$16,000

The Bonner Corporation realizes a $16,000 net dollar benefit from the bank loan at the 12 percent annual rate. However, the firm could easily forfeit that gain if management had focused on the interest rate instead of the net dollar benefit.

To emphasize that fact, let's examine the net annual dollar benefit that would develop for the Bonner Corporation across a range of interest rates:

(1) Annual Interest Rate	(2) Annual Dollar Cost*	(3) Annual Dollar Benefit	(4) Net Gain (3–2)
15%	$10,000	$24,000	$14,000
18%	12,000	24,000	12,000
21%	14,000	24,000	10,000
24%	16,000	24,000	8,000

*Cost of borrowing $66,000 for a full year.

Naturally, the net benefit from the 2 percent cash discounts decreases as the interest rates rise. But, notice the contrast with the common perception. The Bonner Corporation will still realize significant benefits at interest rates that appear exorbitant by traditional standards. The firm's earnings will rise by $8,000 even if it has to pay a 24 percent annual rate for the funds necessary to take the available discounts. The net dollar benefits from a bank loan remain the most important consideration.

Let's look at another illustration that lends support to that claim. That example centers on the potential net dollar benefits a business can gain from using a bank loan to take advantage of quantity discounts some suppliers allow for larger volume purchases. The Assembly Company illustrates that potential.

The Assembly Company manufactures standard desk lamps that have a predictable sales volume of twenty thousand units per year. The company does not produce any of the component parts of the lamps. Instead, it purchases each component from various suppliers.

Using the twenty thousand unit volume as the basis for analysis, the firm projected the potential earnings from using a bank loan to take advantage of discounts allowed for quantity purchases. The analysis began with a look at the quantity discounts offered by the firm's lamp base supplier:

Lot Size	Unit Price
0–1,999	$4.00
2,000–4,999	$3.70
5,000–9,999	$3.40
10,000+	$3.10

The unit purchase price for lamp bases drops from $4.00 to $3.10 when a business increases its order size from 1,999 to 10,000 units.

Beginning with that schedule, the Assembly Company proceeded with the analysis on the following assumptions:

1. The company could make twelve monthly purchases of 1,666 units each or two semi-annual purchases of 10,000 units each.
2. To buy all the lamp bases in a single 20,000 unit order, the company must borrow an average of $20,000 for the year at a 12 percent annual interest rate; that will result in $2,400 in interest costs.

A little arithmetic suggests that the bank loan will lead to some large net dollar benefits for the Assembly Company:

	Annual Purchase Cost Based on Twelve Orders of 1,666 Each	Annual Purchase Cost Based on Two Orders of 10,000 Each
Total Units	20,000	20,000
Unit Cost	$ 4.00	$ 3.10
Total Purchase Costs	$80,000	$62,000
Interest Costs	—	$ 2,400

	Annual Purchase Cost Based on Twelve Orders of 1,666 Each	Annual Purchase Cost Based on Two Orders of 10,000 Each
Total Costs	$80,000	$64,400
Net Benefit from Bank Loan	—	$15,600

Using a bank loan to finance large quantity purchases produces a $15,600 net dollar increase in earnings for the Assembly Company.

However, to emphasize the perspective here, the firm would still enjoy a significant gain even if the bank charged 50 percent for its loan. At that exorbitant rate, the business still would realize an $8,000 net gain from the bank loan.

Again, this emphasizes that the interest rate is irrelevant in evaluating the benefits expected from a bank loan. The proper evaluation weighs the dollar benefits from a loan against the dollar cost. A significant net dollar gain justifies using a bank loan whatever the stated interest rate.

As another example, let's consider the potential benefits from using a bank loan to make purchases that anticipate supplier price hikes. In such instances, the profit comes from the cost savings the business enjoys until it exhausts its supply of the lower priced inventory.

For example, assume a business sells a popular product for $20.00 per case. The firm pays the manufacturer $12.00 per case, enjoying an $8.00 gross margin for each sale.

The manufacturer's sales representative tells the manager that the case price for the product will soon rise by $1.50, i.e., to $13.50. The effective date of the increase remains uncertain, but the hike appears inevitable.

So, the business explored the potential benefits from anticipatory purchasing-buying excess inventory before the price increase. Specifically, the firm considered buying two thousand cases, enough for six month's sales.

However, the business now employs the maximum amount of trade credit approved by the manufacturer. Buying the two thousand cases will require a $24,000 bank loan. The firm initially balked when the bank indicated that, for whatever reason, the loan would carry a

20 percent interest rate. But, further analysis suggests that the high interest rate should not affect the borrowing decision. That analysis compared the dollar benefits from the anticipatory purchase with the dollar cost of the borrowed funds.

Note that the loan will have only a six-month life, i.e., the time necessary to sell the product obtained in the anticipatory buy. The business will reduce the loan at a regular rate as it sells the product. That means that the average loan for the six month period will fall to $12,000.

You find the actual dollar cost for the $12,000 average loan balance with the following calculation:

$$\$12,000 \quad \text{x} \quad 20\% \quad \text{x} \quad 1/2 \quad = \quad \$1,200$$

Although the bank charges a 20 percent annual interest rate, the business pays only $1,200 for the funds necessary to finance the anticipatory purchase. Since that buy will save the business $3,000 (2,000 cases x $1.50 per case saving), the firm's net gain becomes:

Purchase cost savings	$3,000
Borrowing cost	$1,200
Net Gain	$1,800

A lower interest rate on the borrowed funds would increase the benefit from the anticipatory purchase. But, not proceeding with the anticipatory purchase because a banker quotes a high interest rate eliminates that benefit. Again, the net dollar benefit from a bank loan should stand as the focal point of the borrowing decision process.

Achieving a Profitable Level of Operations

On occasion, a tight cash flow stands as the only obstacle to a firm's profitability. A bank loan may provide the financial lubrication necessary to overcome that obstacle. Again, the interest rates in such instances becomes irrelevant. The net earnings that result from the bank loan should be the focus of the borrowing decision process. A look at the Bayline Corporation helps illustrate that fact.

> **Bank Note No. 69:**
> A bank loan may provide the cash a business needs to achieve a profitable sales volume.

The Bayline Corporation now generates a $25,000 monthly sales volume. However, that volume leaves the business with only break-even operating results. At that volume, the firm neither makes nor loses any money.

Of course, the break-even results show that Bayline's monthly costs also total $25,000. That becomes more relevant when we break that total into its fixed and variable components.

Bayline's variable costs, i.e., those that fluctuate in line with sales, average $.60 out of each sales dollar. That means that $15,000 out of the $25,000 monthly total now represents variable costs. Logically, we can assume that the $10,000 difference represents Bayline's monthly fixed costs. Those costs remain constant whatever the firm's monthly sales volume.

The existing cost structure suggests that increasing sales above the $25,000 monthly level will make the business profitable. Each incremental sales dollar over that total will produce a $.40 profit. That acknowledges the $.60 average product cost incurred from each sale. As suggested above, a sales increase will not affect the firm's fixed cost. So, the $.40 difference proceeds directly to the firm's earnings.

Unfortunately, the current $25,000 sales volume is the maximum possible in the firm's present financial circumstances. We do not need to look at the current balance sheet to verify those facts. Merely note that increasing the monthly sales volume from $25,000 to $30,000 will require a $15,000 bank loan. Moreover, that loan will carry an exorbitant 30 percent annual interest rate.

In normal circumstances, a 30 percent annual interest rate will come as an unsettling thought. But, ignore the interest rate and focus on the profitable benefits that can come from the borrowed funds.

The business will gain the financial capacity to increase its sales by $5,000 per month. After using $.60 out of each sales dollar to pay product costs, the firm will have $2,000 per month, or $24,000 per year, to pay for the borrowed funds.

Of course, the 30 percent annual interest rate will make the cost of borrowing $4,500 ($15,000 x 30%). That still leaves the business with $19,500 in new earnings.

Moreover, those results again show that interest rates should not be the central consideration in a borrowing decision. That decision should center on the net dollar benefits that develop from a business loan. A business manager who refuses to borrow because a lender quotes a high rate of interest makes an expensive financial mistake.

Index

Bold entries denote pages with tables or charts. Italicized entries denote pages with illustrations or figures.